PORTRAIT OF

THE LIVERPOOL OVERHEAD RAILWAY

ADRIAN JARVIS

IAN ALLAN *Publishing*

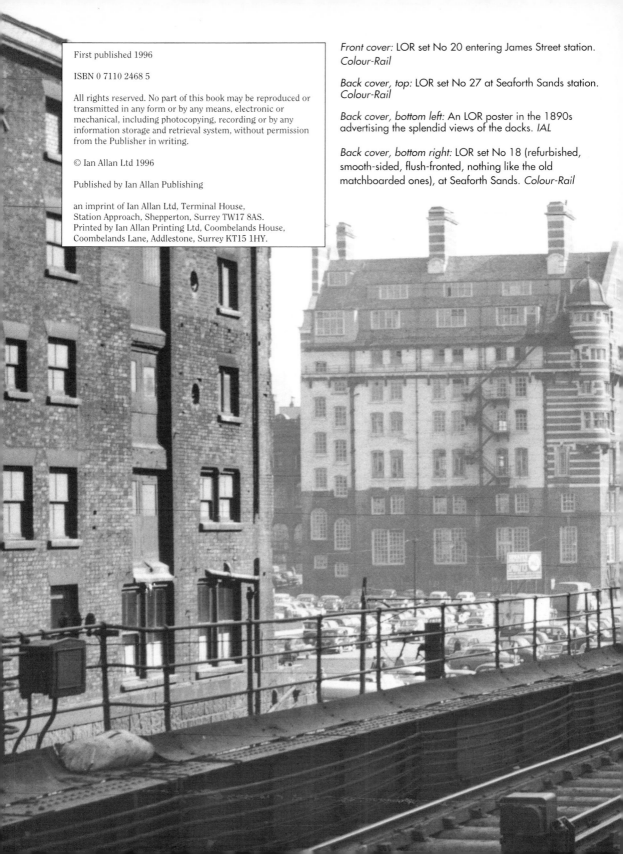

First published 1996

ISBN 0 7110 2468 5

Published by Ian Allan Publishing

an imprint of Ian Allan Ltd, Terminal House,
Station Approach, Shepperton, Surrey TW17 8AS.
Printed by Ian Allan Printing Ltd, Coombelands House,
Coombelands Lane, Addlestone, Surrey KT15 1HY.

Front cover: LOR set No 20 entering James Street station.
Colour-Rail

Back cover, top: LOR set No 27 at Seaforth Sands station.
Colour-Rail

Back cover, bottom left: An LOR poster in the 1890s
advertising the splendid views of the docks. *IAL*

Back cover, bottom right: LOR set No 18 (refurbished,
smooth-sided, flush-fronted, nothing like the old
matchboarded ones), at Seaforth Sands. *Colour-Rail*

Contents

Preface

My first contact with the LOR was being taken for a ride on it as a child, not very long before it closed. Unfortunately, the older cousin who took me was interested in ships, not railways, so my recollection of the railway itself is vague. I next encountered it soon after starting as a trainee in what was then the City of Liverpool Museums, when the land transport gallery was being planned: the Museum had motor coach No 3, one of the colour-light signals, a

Left: An early LOR poster: even at that date the 'Magnificent Panoramic View' was considered a selling point. The train is one of the second batch, with full-width cab, so the passengers could not be alongside the driver as shown. *IAL*

Below: I found this photograph captioned 'The final touches being applied to the paintwork of a rebuilt train in the carriage works of the Liverpool Overhead Railway.' A revisionist interpretation asks why the body panels have been nicely painted and varnished before sending some oaf to splash white roof paint over them. The original caption implies correct workshop practice, which is not what the photograph shows. *C. P. Boocock*

number of minor items and some ephemera and photographs. When it came to researching back-up material for the display of No 3, we did what everybody else did at the time and relied on the one and only book on the subject, namely C. E. Box, *The Liverpool Overhead Railway*, first published in 1957.

In 1982, I was approached by Ian Allan Ltd with a proposal to assist with a new edition of the book. Box was an engineer, and he wrote using mainly engineering sources so that his book, although a splendid record of the railway, was not always easy reading for the layman. My brief was to make it easier and to put in rather more contextual material to 'humanise' the story a bit. Charles Box was a charming and immensely knowledgeable man with whom I had several fascinating discussions of draft material I had produced, but sadly he died on Christmas Eve 1982, when only a couple of new chapters had been completed. I continued alone, and the new edition appeared in 1984.

During 1993, National Museums & Galleries on Merseyside (successors to the City of Liverpool Museums) organised a Research Day School, in collaboration with the University of Liverpool, at

which some new information on the Overhead appeared, and two other papers were given which put the railway more firmly in its technological context. Late in 1994, I was approached by Ian Allan Ltd again: the 1984 edition of Box was sold out and a new account of the LOR was contemplated.

The result is a bit different from many of the *Portrait* series, for the obvious reason that the LOR was a bit different from any other railway. The route was short, totalling only just over seven miles including its extensions; its connections with other railways were unimportant, and its traffic was based on a very large number of passengers paying on average, low fares. Much of its interest and importance lay in its ground-breaking technology. Its building, operation and eventual closure were probably more bedevilled by political (rather than transport) considerations than almost any other line. Compared with most railways, its customer base, rooted in the business of the port, was not so much changeable as positively volatile.

The book also sets out to be mildly revisionist. Box's engineering background and sources, coupled with

his love of the railway and the fact that his father had worked for the LOR from 1911–43, (the last 10 years as General Manager and Engineer) effectively made his an insider account. Insiders have access to useful information, but the danger is that they will see the Company as always being in the right. In a number of cases it appears that the Company was not necessarily behaving wisely or even honestly, and I have sought to draw attention to these in the interests of a more balanced view. This is not intended as destructive criticism: we see incompetence and dishonesty in present-day life and business and to assume that things in the past were not only better put perfect distorts our view of the present and the future as well as of the past. Things don't change all that much: there have always been good and bad businessmen, and ugly ones too. The recognition of this need take nothing away from the positive achievements of the people concerned. I have, for example, been pretty rude about S. B. Cottrell and the Accelerated Service: this does not mean that Cottrell was a Very Bad Engineer. What it means is that he was not invariably 100% right — and which of us is?

A Note about Picture Captions
The problem with the LOR is that an impoverished little company only rarely commissioned a professional photographer and, of course, the amateur shots which survive necessarily date from the period when an f6.3 Nettar was a pretty decent lens. Many of the captions required the use of a magnifying glass to study detail which in some cases is visible in print only with the eye of faith. When, for example on page 71, I state that holes have been drilled in Lively Polly's buffer beam, I simply have to ask the reader to trust me.

Acknowledgements
A number of people have made the writing of this book much easier than it might have been. My colleague Gordon Read, Curator of Archives, National Museums & Galleries on Merseyside and his assistant, Dawn Littler, have saved me a great deal of time by allowing me the privilege of browsing in their stacks. I have not inserted footnotes, but I hope I have made it clear in the text where I am indebted to the work of others, particularly my fellow-contributors to the Research Day School, John Hughes, Michael Duffy, Gordon Woodward and Bruce Maund (in order of their contributions on the day). Behind many a book stands a spouse who does not complain about the mess in the study or the tap that is still awaiting a new washer, and my wife Anthea deserves full acknowledgement of her forebearance. Finally, I would like to thank Peter Waller of Ian Allan Ltd for believing in the project and for not complaining about the extreme age of the computer software I use!

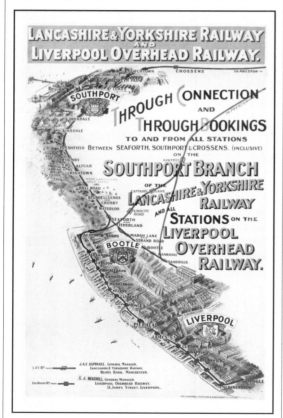

Poster from c1910 advertising the LOR and its through connections. *IAL*

A Need, Some Answers and Some Politics

The Liverpool waterfront in 1850 was an exceedingly busy place. Liverpool was the second largest port in the world, and the nature of the Mersey estuary had forced successive dock engineers to construct their docks in a long narrow line, mostly built out from the old shoreline into the river. Approximately along that old shoreline ran a road which had many different names at different parts of its length — Chaloner Street, Wapping, Strand, New Quay, Waterloo Road and more — which became known, as it is still known today, as 'The Dock Road'.

The 1840s had witnessed an explosion of activity along the Liverpool waterfront, which had two different and interdependent causes. The first, and more generally known, was the result of the Industrial Revolution in inland Lancashire, which had become the world centre of cotton milling and a very important centre of such related industries as mill machinery construction. Both these main branches had numerous ancillaries such as dyeing and printing of textiles on the one hand and engine and boiler manufacture on the other. Taken together, these things made Lancashire the centre of the largest ocean-borne trade the world had ever seen, and Liverpool was the port which handled almost all of it.

That much you could learn, between yawns, from any standard textbook written for economic history students. There was, however, more to it than that. In 1824, the Liverpool Dock Trustees had finally got rid of their very able but totally corrupt Dock Surveyor, John Foster, and replaced him with an untested bridge engineer named Jesse Hartley. He was a man who wanted control of everything he was involved with, and he gradually built up an unprecedented integrated engineering establishment rather like that of Crewe Works — but he did it in the late 1820s, rather before the Johnny-come-lately railway industry. He built himself a position of enormous power, in which he was paid more than the next three highest paid officers of the Dock Trustees put together and about four times as much as a typical chief engineer of a major railway company. It is symptomatic that his office was not in the Dock Offices, but in his 'Dock Yard' (engineer's depot): you wanted to do business with Mr Hartley, you went to him.

But however important he was, in one sense he was just a very expensive hired hand. The other half of the business was, for a time, his fellow Yorkshireman John Bramley-Moore, who had started his working life as an office junior in a merchant's office in Brazil at the age of about 14. In 1843, he became Chairman of the Dock Committee, and for five years an amazing partnership ruled the port. Hartley was the most prolific and successful dock engineer in the world, and the only man who had even higher ambitions for Liverpool was Bramley-Moore. One delivered the money, the other the docks and the trade, and the result was that Liverpool both outgrew and outdistanced every competitor. It became by far the largest port in the world to be run by a single authority. When the Dock Trustees were abolished by the Mersey Docks & Harbour Board Act of 1857, it was not for corruption or ineptitude, but for doing their job so well and making so much money as to arouse the jealousy of powerful commercial interests which plotted their downfall.

Hartley's Albert Dock warehouses are now among the country's top tourist attractions, and anyone remotely interested in industrial archaeology will soon find the similar blocks he built at Wapping and Stanley. But in the longer story of the port these were a brief deviation: from the beginning, public general warehouses had been built close to, but not on, the Dock Estate. This meant that nearly all the goods going to or from the quays were transported a short distance by horse-drawn carts. In 1850, some 3.5 million tons of shipping entered Liverpool. Because of the way tonnage was measured, the actual tonnage of goods was around 1.5 times the nominal tonnage of the vessels. Let us allow that some may have come in with ballast and say that somewhere about 4.5 million tons of cargo were discharged. A typical cart carried about 15cwt, so that the import cargoes would represent, very roughly, six million cartloads. Then the ships had to be loaded with their export cargoes…

No records survive which tell us how many carts there were on the Dock Road, or how many trips per day they made. What we do know is that one obvious reason why there should not be nearly so many as we think — namely the removal of goods directly by railway or canal — does not account for much. Direct canal connection had been resisted until 1848, and long after that the Harbourmaster tried to prevent too many grubby little boats getting in among his nice ships and messing up his system by taking goods overside instead of from quays. The Dock Trustees got on extremely badly with railway companies from the days of the Liverpool & Manchester Railway onwards. Hartley was all in favour of railways, but only when he controlled them: the idea of letting large powerful companies onto his territory very definitely did not appeal, and that was a view in which his Committee supported him to the hilt.

The result was congestion on the Dock Road which was serious by the standards of modern rush hours. The dockers were not employed by the Dock Trustees, but by small firms of Master Stevedores or Master Porters, whose records have not survived, but we know the number of men they employed ran into five digits. Then there was our friend Mr Hartley again: he was always either building something new or reconstructing something obsolete, and he usually had a thousand or so men, whether his own or contractors', working somewhere along the Dock Road. At really busy times they numbered up to about 4,000. They were sending out spoil from excavations by the hundred thousand tons per year, and receiving construction materials in equally large quantities. Much of this extra 'cargo' came and went by boat, but some added to the mayhem along the Dock Road.

But the Dock Road was not just a hideously overcrowded route for goods and for men working on the docks. It was much more complicated, busy and confused than that. Along its inland side and in the side streets lay a multitude of railway depots, bonded warehouses and forwarding depots. There were many other businesses: export packers, ship repairers and provision merchants. There were factories too, mainly in the heavy process industries that tend to gather in ports, like seed oil pressing and sugar refining. All of these added to the press of people and goods on the Dock Road.

Another major traffic was in emigrants, who passed through Liverpool in their thousands every year, bound for a new life in America, Australia or wherever. These generated their own infrastructure of provision merchants (steerage passengers had to find their own food) and a host of assorted spivs and con-men offering 'valuable services' to suckers who were overwhelmed by their first encounter with a great port. Hotels of varying degrees of squalor served both the emigrants and the less important commercial visitors.

We often assume that bureaucracy is a modern invention. A look along the Dock Road in 1850 would show it is not, for among the endless hurrying people were a small army of clerks, messengers and other assorted minions. Consider what happened when a ship arrived in port: it had to be entered with HM Customs, it had to pay Dock Dues, it had to find someone to discharge its cargo. It very likely needed

to go into graving dock for a quick check-up and the removal of marine growth from its bottom. Each of these steps was highly complicated. Customs procedures were, by this time, becoming simpler but still involved the verification of the exact weight and nature of the cargo. What I have cheerfully called 'Dock Dues' were in fact made up of three separate charges: harbour dues payable on the register tonnage of the ship, dock dues, and town dues payable on the tonnage of the cargo. These latter naturally depended on the nature of the goods, and lengthy tables of rates were printed; the categories into which goods fitted were not the same as the categories used either by Customs or by the contractors to whom we come next. Goods were broken out from the hold and hoisted to the ship's side by 'lumpers', at which point they became the responsibility of 'porters'. In some cases these separate groups of men worked for the same firm; in others they did not.

And so it went on: we have yet to account for services like weighing or bagging of goods which were provided by the Dock Trustees. A particularly choice bit of bureaucracy arose with the bushelling (ie measuring by volume) of grain: the charge for the service was made not by the bushel but by the ton! Then came the consignees who wanted to know that they had not been cheated by any of the others (leaving bales of cotton standing in the rain before weighing them was a tried and tested ploy), the carters and the warehousemen.

Then there were the pubs and beerhouses, mostly small, but very numerous. They were not just places where people went to relax or to drink away their problems: they were places where a good deal of business got done. If a captain needed to find some painters in a hurry, the men at the graving docks would be able to tell him which pubs the painters went in. To the lowlier members of the Liverpool shipping community they fulfilled the functions of a gentleman's club. To the sailors, many of whom had a few days available in which to spend their entire earnings from the last couple of months on what we may politely style 'a good time', they fulfilled a different role.

Taken together, the quantity of people and goods seeking to use the Dock Road made it a place of congestion, delay and danger, to say nothing of rage, fury and rude words. It seemed, in short, to be just the place where a railway could make a lot of money by solving a lot of people's problems.

The first scheme was proposed by an engineer named John Grantham, in a paper read to the Liverpool Polytechnic Society (of which he was a founder member) in 1853. What he envisaged was a high-level railway with storage accommodation underneath, which sounds, at first hearing, an absolutely daft idea. Perhaps it was, but the existing

Right: A view of the Overhead soon after opening. In the left foreground is one of the 'tramnibuses' still on the road. There are two topsail schooners in George's Dock and the paint on Pier Head station still looks fit for a Prime Ministerial visit. *IAL*

Right: Another view of Pier Head station taken about the same time. This shows the attempt to make Pier Head a stylish station by means of a portal arch echoing that at Seaforth Sands. The overall roof which that implies was not, of course, provided.

Below: This rather later view shows the foundation and basement works of the Cunard Building under construction in the foreground and the Goree Warehouses beyond the railway. *IAL*

Above: Princes Dock station, prior to 1900, and typical of LOR structures. Note the centre 'third' conductor rail.

constraints provide some excuse. The boundary of the Dock Estate was marked by a high wall, originally at the behest of HM Customs, for most of its length. Outside the wall lay Hartley's 'Dock Line of Railway' which acted as a spine from which branches turned off for the various docks and into the equally various railway yards. There was no ground-level space available, therefore one had to go upwards or downwards. The latter was, quite rightly, not considered a sensible option. It is worth recalling in passing that Grantham was an engineer of great versatility and some importance in canal, marine and railway engineering. He can certainly not be dismissed along with some of the nutters who wrote to the Trustees claiming to know the answers to all of Liverpool's problems. The unworthy thought has occurred to the author that Grantham might have imagined that just because Hartley was 73, there might be a very well-paid job going. If he did, he was wide of the mark. Smiles may tell us of wimps like Brindley or Brunel who worked themselves to an early grave, but Jesse was made of sterner stuff than that and worked until he was 80.

Grantham proposed a logical solution, which was to build a goods railway mainly on the tops of transit sheds. But this meant an intrusion onto the Dock Estate, which Jesse Hartley was scarcely likely to welcome with open arms. Later in 1853, the response came in a pamphlet by Jesse and his son (and deputy) John Bernard, entitled Report of the Dock Surveyors on a Proposed Plan of High level Railway upon the Quays of the Liverpool Docks. It was a pretty ferocious attack, which explained the rationale of cargo handling in the docks and showed that Grantham's scheme would foul everything up.

Hartley is often thought, from this and similar attacks on railway projects, to have been anti-railway. He was nothing of the kind: in a drawing of 1845, authorised with his signature, lines are shown serving virtually every quay in the port. What Hartley was against, and very strongly against, was lines which were not under his control from conception to operation. The Grantham scheme, being someone else's idea, got off to a bad start.

Grantham was not privy to what else Hartley was planning at the time. His 1855 Dock Bill, which failed in Parliament through the activities of the Birkenhead lobby, included large new docks on the inland side of the Dock Road, which would have required large movable bridges, at what was then the sharp end of technology, to allow ships to pass the proposed railway. Even worse, the Bill included proposals for huge blocks of warehouses at Princes and Waterloo which were quite incompatible with the 'shed-top' idea.

There was no way Hartley was going to allow himself to be circumscribed: over the disposition of railways on the Dock Estate his pen was law.

The priorities of the Grantham scheme had been, in one sense, the right way round, for it had sought to give unimpeded facilities for goods up aloft, leaving the people to take their chance below. The next two attempted solutions approached the problem the other way around: passengers were lighter than goods, so it should be the passengers that went aloft, not the goods. An engineer named Sharpe proposed a railway which would leave what is now the Merseyrail line from Southport at Marsh Lane, Bootle and make its way at high level along the line of docks to a point near the bottom of Chapel Street. In the light of the basic needs explained above, and the customer base of the Overhead as explained below, this scheme seems to have lacked market research, or 'traffic taking' as it was then called. The congestion was along the whole length of the Dock Road, and this route ran only about halfway.

The man whose vision of the Overhead both addressed the basic problems, and found the bones of what would be the successful answer, was Alfred Holt. He is principally remembered for opening up the Far East to the steam cargo liner trade, but he was a man of many parts, several of which deserve to be better known. He started his working life as an apprentice to Edward Woods, Chief Engineer to the Liverpool & Manchester Railway, where he is said to have 'received a thorough grounding in both civil and mechanical aspects of railway engineering'. He was duly elected a Member of the Institution of Civil Engineers. Although he was not elected to the Mersey Docks & Harbour Board until 1867, seven years after Hartley's retirement, he shared and perpetuated Hartley's view that railways were a good thing, but railway companies an exceedingly bad one. In 1877, he proposed that the Board should build an overhead passenger tramway in order to leave ground level free for goods.

Behind this proposal lay the difficulties which had been occurring with omnibuses. Two companies had been leased the right to run rather curious vehicles we might call 'tramnibuses' on Hartley's Dock Line of Railway. These vehicles were horse-drawn, and ran on the railway lines until they encountered horse-drawn (or parked) goods wagons, upon which they derailed themselves and drove along on the setts until past the obstruction, when they re-railed. Although they ran at a frequency of every 3 or 4min, they were incapable either of carrying everyone who wanted to travel or of avoiding obstruction to goods traffic. Even more were they incapable of working to the satisfaction of the Dock Board, with the result that in the early 1860s around half of all the weekly meetings of the Works Committee (of the Board) had their agendas ornamented with alleged 'irregularities' perpetrated by the tramnibuses. None of this really mattered anyway: they carried a couple of dozen people at 4mph at ground level. Although they totalled around 1.5 million passengers per year, that was never going to be enough to have any real impact on the congestion and overcrowding.

The situation on the rails was made more difficult by the fact that the goods traffic mostly continued until 1895 in the pattern set by Hartley. He did not want locomotives or sizeable trains on his railway,

which sounds archaic but was actually quite a clever policy when he adopted it. Wagons were to be drawn singly or in twos and threes by horses. It meant he could employ tight curves and avoid the need for complex sidings arrangements on the congested Dock Estate — it was for the railway companies to tie up their land marshalling trains. Horses also had the considerable advantage that where any shunting was needed they could walk across the tracks, after the manner of the Hornby 'air-shunting' of our childhood. So long as distances were short and gradients negligible horses were an appropriate technology. The trouble with them, for present purposes, was that because the 'trains' were very small, the number of 'train movements' on the Dock Line was necessarily large, whence came much of the conflict with the tramnibuses.

Although Holt's engineering education was of a pretty conventional nature, he was a man of original ideas. In 1881, he gave a paper to the Liverpool Engineering Society in which he described progress on the scheme for an overhead railway. At a political level, what he proposed was a doubtful venture, for the railway was to be built and operated by the Dock Board. That august body of men had been established, we recall, to carry on the successes of the old Trustee body without upsetting its customers by being too good at it. Its Act stated that 'Save as by this Act is provided, no Moneys receivable by the Board shall be applied to any Purpose unless the same conduces to the Safety or Convenience of Ships frequenting the Port of Liverpool or facilitates the shipping or unshipping of Goods or is concerned in discharging a Debt contracted for the above Purposes.' Now it could be, and was, argued that the provision of a passenger railway would facilitate the shipping and unshipping of goods, but some members of the Board felt that it would be at best a dilution of their effort in their main business and at worst illegal.

At a practical level, the proposal was more likely to gain credence than Grantham's had been, for there was by now an elevated railway operating in New York. It featured an economy measure which was to become a special love of Holt's, namely that by operating at relatively low speed it was able to dispense with signalling systems entirely. It is clear that what Holt envisaged was completely different from what the Overhead eventually became: he proposed steam-heated carriages which were to be quite luxuriously fitted out: they were obviously intended more for carrying the small armies of business users than the larger ones of dock labourers. His initial arithmetic on capital and running costs suggested the line could more than pay for itself even if it raised no more revenue than the tramnibuses did. The Board therefore agreed, despite a few reservations, that G. F. Lyster, their

Engineer-in-Chief, should prepare a report, with more detailed plans and estimates. Lyster was already grooming his son Anthony to become his successor (which he eventually did in 1897), and dispatched him to the USA to observe and record a number of things at which Americans were thought to be good, notably bulk grain handling systems and urban railways — particularly the new elevated railway in New York. When Lyster Junior returned with his findings, traffic in New York was booming and enthusiasm for the Liverpool scheme was riding high.

Lyster Senior followed the Holt view that a single track would be sufficient, particularly on account of the abolition of signalling costs, and the first scheme produced was on that basis. The Board of Trade, via Colonel Yolland, showed a marked lack of enthusiasm for the single-track proposal, so Lyster was asked to draw up a scheme for a double-track line. There was probably a bit of politicking going on here: Holt was strongly in favour of the single-track signal-free scheme which John Hughes has shown would have allowed some very dangerous situations to arise. Holt had previously campaigned hard and successfully against the Board of Trade on the issue of the maximum permissible pressures of marine boilers, so the double-track argument may have been the BoT's way of attempting to avoid another head-to-head with Holt. There followed an extraordinary sequence of comings and goings, including a complete volte-face by the BoT, which resulted in a new set of estimates which were approaching four times Holt's original ballpark figure of £150,000.

The first Act enabling the railway had been passed in 1878, but by 1885 nothing had appeared on the ground apart from a couple of (full-size) trial spans which Lyster had his men construct in the Dock Yard, and which were scrapped in 1881. By 1885, Lyster was beginning to get worried: the latest figures he had worked out suggested that for the railway to meet its operating cost and pay the interest on its capital — let alone produce any profit — it would need to carry some eight million passengers per year. Clearly the potential total traffic was growing, and the improved service which would be possible with an elevated railway might cause it to grow more, but the need to quintuple the existing traffic to reach break-even point was not encouraging.

The politics were very complicated. The Members of the Board were not, theoretically, representatives of particular interests or trades, but in fact they often acted that way. Lyster was engaged in a huge programme of dock expansion which was enabled under an Act of 1873, but which had the curious rider that he was not allowed to spend more than £500,000 of the enabled capital in any one year. This was one of the reasons why the programme was not

completed until 1888. It involved the extension of the Dock Estate further to the north by the construction of the docks from Canada to Alexandra and the considerable expansion of the docks near the south end, with the construction of Toxteth and Harrington. These extensions had been achieved in the face of fierce opposition from the Birkenhead lobby both within and outside the Board, and there was no doubt that any failure of the new docks to deliver the goods would be joyously pounced upon.

It was well known to both sides in the dispute that the reason the Birkenhead Docks had, thus far, been such a poor investment was that they were remote and inconvenient for the conduct of 'business in person' by the armies of messengers, clerks and occasional more important people. As the Liverpool Docks extended further away from the mercantile heart of the town, they might suffer the same problem of unpopularity with customers. The putative Overhead Railway was, therefore, a potentially important component in an altogether bigger game. In that bigger game, which bore on Liverpool's competitive position in the worldwide port services industry, the half a million or so involved was a piddling sum. Any reader who has served on any committee of or for practically anything will recognise, however, that the piddlingness of the sum bears no relationship to the amount of time which its consideration will absorb.

There had already been offers to solve this problem for the Board: sympathetic individuals like Thomas Ismay and William Forwood had more than once offered to float a company to build and operate the Overhead. To the average reader, innocent of Liverpool's commercial politics and probably picturing benign and whiskery Victorian gents reminiscent of Old Jolyon Forsyte, this doubtless sounds a good idea. Members reacted with suspicion. The obvious reason for their looking this apparent gift horse in the mouth was the legacy of Hartley: they did not want a railway on their Estate unless it was under their control. A slightly less obvious reason is that in 1880, Ismay had proposed a magnificent cost-saving scheme for the Port. He would abolish all dues on goods, and make dues payable only on the ships which carried them, which would save enormous amounts of administration and would bring great benefits to merchants and brokers, whose cash flow would be helped by not having to lay out dues in advance of receipt of their money. There was just one slight catch in this splendid idea: Members of the Board were elected by Dock Electors, and Dock Electors were those who paid Dues: Ismay's 'magnanimous' suggestion was nothing less than an attempt to disenfranchise the merchants and have the Board constituted entirely of the representatives of shipowners like himself. We may perhaps forgive

Above: The structure in course of erection at Alexandra Dock.

those members of the Board who did not entirely trust him.

There had also been suggestions that the Board might gain the benefits of the railway's construction without involving itself, by doing a deal with a railway contractor who might be able to finance it. Read as it was presented, this sounded a most appealing idea, offering the best of all possible worlds: the Board would own the land on which the railway stood and would thus retain a fair measure of control. It seemed to offer the temptation of power without responsibility. Many of the members, however, knew enough about railway promotion to understand not only the scams which were worked by what became known as "contractors' railways" but also the effect that being seen to be involved in such things might have on the Board's most valuable asset. That asset was not a dock, or a patch of land or a building, but the Board's reputation as a financially sound body governed by men who might

be a little dull and unadventurous but were of unsurpassed probity. If they could not continue to borrow more and more money for new development, the port would be out of business. Sometimes we may get the impression that Members did not know which way was up, but in that respect they knew their business and time would prove them right.

The Act of 1879 had been renewed with minor variations in 1882, but, for the reasons outlined above, nothing much had happened. This second Act was also followed by frenzied inactivity, at least in physical terms. The 1882 scheme was for a conventional dual-track steam-hauled service, though the carriages were to be more like trams than railway carriages. The locomotives were, as Parliamentary draftsmen always stipulated, to be so arranged as effectually to consume their own smoke, which, of course, locomotives never did outside of the Houses of Parliament. The estimated cost was £585,000 — slightly more than Lyster estimated three years later. The important difference between the proposals of 1882 and 1885 is that by 1885 Lyster had firmly thrown his weight behind the electric traction option. Whether that was his own idea is open to some doubt: he may have been talked into it by young Anthony. The fact is that Lyster Senior received by far the largest salary paid to any officer of the Board, and they paid him all that money, £4,500 a year no less, to accept responsibility for the whole of his department if things went wrong. In the absence of firm evidence to the contrary, we must therefore allow him to claim the credit for those things which went well. It eventually proved to be quite a momentous recommendation.

In 1887, the Board took another Bill to Parliament which extended the time limits, made minor variations in the route and empowered the Board to lease the entire project to any limited company. The last provision failed, requiring another trip to London the following year. The 1888 Act allowed the establishment of an Overhead Railway Company which would rent the necessary land and rights from the Board for £1,000 pa and half of any profits beyond 5% (later increased to 6%) on the capital.

The 1888 Act should have been sufficient to allow construction to begin, but we find another Bill in Parliament the following year. It was a surprising Bill, in that instead of being promoted by the new Company which was to build the railway, it was promoted by the Board. We have been led to believe that some Members wanted to control the railway, others to avoid getting involved. It seems that there was another, murkier, desire which came to the surface over the issue of what appears at first sight to be a minor variation in the route. The 1889 proceedings are strange in a number of ways, of which the strangest is that the newly-formed Company was able, before a rivet had been closed, to extract concessions from the mighty MD&HB. Were there, perhaps, things going on beneath the surface which were in some ways as important as those being proposed 16ft above it?

The 1888 Act is usually said to have enabled the lease of the Board's powers to build the railway to the Company. In the main it did, but it did not cover all of the powers. The compulsory purchase powers for land needed both for the railway itself and for working sites during construction were retained by the Board. In a sense this was entirely reasonable, for the greater part of the line stood on land to be leased from the Board. The Act also provided powers to vary the line of the Overhead in the section beside Queens and Coburg Docks, and a look at what was happening in that part of the Dock Estate suggests that the Board was looking as much to the operation of the docks as of the railway in seeking these variations.

If one walks along the Dock Road today, its line seems to be obviously and almost naturally governed by the shape of the docks it adjoins. In 1888 the line was different: Chaloner Street, now part of the Dock Road, was in fact the first road inland from a street known, quite descriptively, as 'East Side of Queens Dock'. Between the two lay several small side streets

at right angles to the dock and a host of small businesses dealing in shipping-related goods and services — smithies, cooperages, boatbuilders' shops, pubs, foundries, carters' depots. Useful, perhaps even picturesque to the modern eye, though these businesses might have been, they stood in the way of changing times. The Board was under intense and constant pressure to provide ever more and better space for steamships, which both loaded and discharged much faster than their sail-powered competitors. Speed of handling demanded a change in the basic proportions of docks: a better quayside to waterspace ratio and more quay area to quay length. Queens was a large and obsolescent dock which was to be upgraded for steamship use and as part of that upgrading it needed wider quay margins to accommodate the larger quantities of goods which cascaded at ever-increasing speed from modern steamships.

The Board had been addressing this problem for a year or two. In May 1887 they paid £5,274 for 1,457sq yd of land on Bridgewater Street 'in connection with the proposed arrangements for deepening the water in the Queens Dock'. A sequence of small properties was acquired at prices averaging around £3–£4 per sq yd. The occupants of other properties in the vicinity were soon able to work out what was going on, and thus held out for ever-higher prices. Within a few months the Board was having to pay twice as much. There was an easier way to acquire the necessary land, and that was to use the compulsory powers granted for the building of the Overhead, which was duly diverted straight through the properties of those who were holding out for rip-off prices from the Board.

As we follow the story of the construction of the Overhead, we shall find that the Dock Board, which generally loathed railway companies, treated the Overhead in a very different way. Seen from the other side, the Company dealt with the Board in a manner suggesting that it had real negotiating power. As a somewhat piddling company in which the Board had a reasonable holding of shares and the right to nominate one director, it might be expected to be in a weak position. It proved not to be so, and the reason was that if the Company needed the Board to provide its route and its financial credibility, the Board had found what we might politely term extra-legal benefits which it could derive from the activities of the Company. More bluntly, it was using Parliamentary powers granted for building the railway to enable what it considered vital improvements to the dock system. It was probably right to do so, but what it did was illegal. Laying oneself open to blackmail was not necessarily the wisest thing to do when one's 'partners' were such forceful men as Forwood, the Company Chairman, or Alsop, the Company Solicitor.

Chapter 2

The Design Problems and the Technology

The whole need for an overhead railway arose from the lack of space at ground level, so an overhead railway built, like many of the lines into Manchester, on brick arches was out of the question. The original Grantham proposal was simply an inversion of this technology: instead of speaking of a viaduct with arch storage space underneath, one spoke of sheds with a railway on top. What's in a name? Either way there was going to be both an obstruction to traffic at ground level and an impediment to the constant change which had to go on within the Dock Estate to enable it to meet the continually varying demands imposed on it by the changing trades of its customers.

At one stage in his contemplation of the Overhead, Alfred Holt was of the opinion that the Overhead could be built on a metal decking with one side resting on columns and the other on the boundary wall of the estate. If we look at Hartley's mighty granite walls from the outside, that seems like an excellent money-saving idea, but if we go to one of the gateways in them and look at the ends of the wall, it becomes clear that here, as in his retaining walls, Hartley actually built rather economically: his granite walling is thinner at the top than the four-course brick walls used at both earlier and later dates. Good though they were, putting a railway on them might have been a little rash.

The railway therefore needed to stand on metal stilts of one form or another. Making columns which would withstand the straightforward vertical loadings and transfer them to foundation blocks or piles was easy enough. Unfortunately, by no means all of the forces involved in running a railway act vertically, or can easily be made to do so. Sideways forces on a metal viaduct were likely to necessitate diagonal braces between the legs, which would make the metal structure just as unacceptable as a brick one would have been, and for the same reasons: that the space below could not carry on with its goods traffic as if nothing had happened.

In these circumstances, steam locomotives were a bad idea for several reasons. Rope haulage had become quite a highly-developed technology in the new guise of the street cable-car, and it removed the weight of the prime mover from the track altogether. Electric traction offered a half-way house, in that the coal and the boilers were left behind and only the electric motor, which was comparatively light, had to travel. Just in terms of weight, steam was the loser. But it went further than that, for there was the hammer-blow effect to take into account, which could double the peak axle loading of a given locomotive.

These forces were the easy ones to deal with, for they acted downwards. The Overhead as proposed

Left: The original pattern collector shoe, as used with the centre conductor rail.

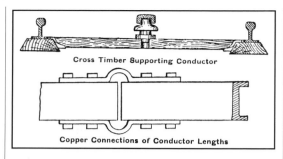

Details of the conductor rail arrangement.

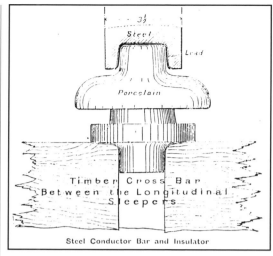

Steel Conductor Bar and Insulator

would involve trains spending virtually none of their time at steady speed: with many of the stations only about a quarter of a mile apart and some even less, they would be almost always either accelerating or braking. That Newton fellow, who fouled up so many good practical ideas with his tiresome theories, could tell us that the acceleration and braking forces would tend to rick the structure longitudinally. If the service was to attain an acceptable average speed over the full length of the route, then the rates of acceleration and deceleration would need to be quite high. The steam locomotives developed in America for high-frequency urban services accelerated remarkably rapidly (nearing 2ft/sec²) but obviously to achieve this they needed to be both powerful and heavy, thus increasing the forces on the structure. Nearer home, the Mersey Railway locomotives (which admittedly had to overcome some dire gradients as well) achieved quite impressive acceleration — but only at the expense of weighing over 60 tons.

The idea of depicting a railway system in a stylised layout plan which is not to scale is usually attributed to the London Underground. A Tube map tends to make us forget that what appears on the map as straight is no more straight than the jellied eels that the people who live down there profess to enjoy eating. So it was with the Overhead: it looked lovely and straight on the diagram in the carriages, but in fact a significant proportion of its length was on curves. When a train went round a corner, it did so because it was constrained by the track, despite its desire to observe the Second Law of Motion by carrying straight on. The force resulting from the defeat of the Second Law tried to rick the structure sideways. Reduction of the weight of the trains was thus a matter of considerable importance in the overall cost of the undertaking.

There were other reasons for avoiding the use of steam locomotives, should it prove possible. The perpetuation of horse traction for most of the traffic on the Dock Line of Railway arose only in part from the factors mentioned in Chapter 1: many of the largest and longest-standing trades through Liverpool were in things which burned rather well, like cotton, sugar and rum. The fear of fire was profound — and justifiable. When the Board was doing its best to avoid the use of steam traction at ground level, it was scarcely likely to wish to adopt it at high level, where there was a risk of hot things falling out of ashpans to be added to what came flying out of chimneys. If there was any acceptable alternative, it was likely to find favour. The problem of smoke pollution was not a very serious one, since most of the route ran through places which were heavily polluted already and noise was probably not much of a worry either. The average locomotive would probably have struggled to make itself heard above the sound of the philosophical discussions among carters on the subject of rights of way. Even so, a quieter and cleaner alternative, while not perhaps a high priority, would be preferable.

Although Michael Faraday had demonstrated an experimental electric motor and dynamo in 1831, it was not really until the 1870s that either device began to show its potential for large-scale development. Once that did begin, however, progress was very rapid, and the first major landmark for our purposes was the little electric railway erected at the Berlin Exhibition of 1879 by Siemens and Halske. Just four years later, the first electrically operated public transport service in Britain, the Portrush to Giant's Causeway tramway, opened for business. The real impetus was built up in America: by the time Sir William Forwood visited America in 1891 there were some 2,500 miles of electric tramways in service. The sheer size of the American market for electric traction was enough to ensure that American electrical engineers would stand a better-than-even chance of becoming world leaders in the field. It was also quite sufficient to

Above: The four original engines and generators. Notice that the power station has plenty of floorspace but little headroom, one reason for adopting this arrangement. In the distance the 'new' (1895) main board can just be seen. *IAL*

convince Forwood that electric traction should be taken very seriously.

This does not mean that there was nothing interesting happening in Britain. The first electric underground railway in the world was the City & South London, opened in 1890. Back in Liverpool, there was nothing doing in the way of electric traction, but the Lysters, both father and son, had been early in the field of using electric arc lamps, supplied by steam-driven Gramme dynamos. Some of the new extension works on the docks had to be carried out in the space of about 2hr at low water of equinoctial spring tides — which gave perhaps 16hr working time per year. The arc lamp doubled this by allowing them to work on the night tides as well. There had been a number of early experiments and demonstrations with electric lighting for other purposes, including one at Lime Street station in

1851 and another at Sandon Graving Docks in 1854, but such schemes were ahead of their time in the sense that no really practical dynamos existed: these earlier lamps relied on primary cells.

By the 1880s, Liverpool was witnessing the beginnings of a public supply system. Holmes & Vaudery, civil engineers, formed the Liverpool Electric Supply Co Ltd in 1883, and built a tiny generating station in Eberle Street, in the heart of the office quarter of town. The company succeeded, and when decision time arrived for the Overhead Railway they had four stations generating and were paying a dividend of 5%. (This sounds modest, but these were recessionary times, and interest rates were low, so 5% was far from bad.)

When an earlier generation of railway pioneers in Liverpool decided that the Liverpool & Manchester Railway would be entirely locomotive-hauled between Manchester and Edge Hill, some at least of the Directors voted for it not so much because it was a visibly superior system, but because it was clearly a technology which was at the beginning of its development rather than the end. Its achievements were not all that great, but its potential was. So it was with the Overhead: electric traction was

Right: One of the keys to the Overhead's technical success — the series/parallel controller shown in a state of undress.

Below: Testing the double-deck swingbridge at Stanley in 1893.

comparatively unproven, but the rate at which it was gaining ground, especially in America, combined with the success of local applications of electric lighting to embolden both Lyster and the advocates of the Overhead project.

Although investigation of alternative modes of traction had been going on for years, and the 1888 Act allowed the use of electric traction, it was not until August 1891 that the Company formally decided upon it. This is an interesting sense of timing, for the erection of the structure had been in hand for rising two years. It was afterwards stated by the engineers for the line that the railway was to be constructed 'at an estimated cost of about £585,000 (subsequently reduced to £466,000 for a system fully equipped and worked by electricity)'. This must mean that the lighter loadings imposed by electric stock allowed the structure to be lighter and cheaper — so to what standard were the engineers working for 21 months when the form of traction had yet to be decided? It seems pretty clear that an effective, and illegal, decision had been taken, pre-empting the views of the Directors, that the railway should be electrically worked.

The obvious precedent to follow was that of the City & South London Railway, which used electric locomotives to haul small trains of conventional carriage stock. Once again, the decision was to opt for potential rather than achievement, in the shape of the 'motor-car'. This relatively untested development of tramcar technology spread its weight much more uniformly along the length of the train, a great advantage when the objective was to save on the cost of an overhead structure. Even the gross weight was reduced considerably: a City & South London train for 96 passengers used a locomotive weighing 10 tons 7cwt, while the electrical equipment for an LOR train carrying 114 people weighed just 6 tons 7cwt. If the railway succeeded in attracting a large traffic, longer trains could be run without increasing axle loadings or loadings per ft run of structure. The steam-hauled New York elevated railways encountered this problem: crowded to bursting point, they reached the limits of locomotive power and of reducing headway.

There already existed, in American practice, some measure of agreement as to traction supply. It should be dc, at what we would now consider a low voltage, namely around 450-500. In the case of 'tube' or overhead railways, where there was no legitimate reason for Joe Public to be on the track to electrocute himself, collection could be by a third-rail pick-up which was cheaper, simpler and more reliable than overhead collectors. The form initially adopted on the LOR was an inverted channel bar in the middle of the track mounted on insulators carried on transverse 'sleepers', the return current being carried by the running rails. The joints in the conductor rail had copper connections, while the running rails had riveted-in iron bonds bridging the fishplates. The prospective earth leakage of this arrangement aroused the ire of Sir William Preece (Postmaster General) who considered that such things interfered with telegraph/telephone cables, but in fact the LOR's leakage was remarkably low and there is no evidence that it did any harm to anyone.

There was nobody in Liverpool generating enough electricity to supply the Overhead, so it had to build its own generating station. The location needed to be somewhere that coal could be directly delivered by rail or, possibly coastal steamer, which was about halfway along the route, and which had access to a dock which could be employed as the condenser cold well. Happily, some of the arches under the High Level Coal Railway were available and were duly leased from the Board for the same rather optimistic term as the route, namely 999 years.

This location met the desiderata very well. The High Level Coal Railway (L&YR) was able to deliver coal in any desired quantity through the boilerhouse roof. In the event that coal from some other part of the country, delivered by coastal steamer, became better value, the dock was just as available for that purpose as it was for providing condenser water. It was substantially nearer to Alexandra than to Herculaneum, but the distances for current supply were deemed acceptable. The Wellington and Bramley-Moore docks were not exactly at the cutting edge either of dock-building technology or of the revenues of the MD&HB. While to the Company it was an almost ideal site, to the Board it was a site in the second rank for which any remunerative use would be reasonably welcome. The Board was, as mentioned in Chapter 1, extremely accommodating.

The machinery which the LOR chose to instal is interesting as an illustration of the need to strike a balance between innovation and best practice. Having taken the slightly risky decision to go for innovation both in the structure and in the use of electric traction, they understandably chose risk limitation in the power station. They could have employed the extremely sophisticated Willans direct-coupled central-valve engines which were fast catching on for electricity generation and which became the standard prime mover for the majority of municipal power stations in the late 1890s and beyond. Had they been really adventurous, the Parsons turbine was already available. But innovation is always risky and expensive, and the Company presumably thought it was taking enough risks already. It was decided that the generators would be driven by variants of the Lancashire mill engine, and the order was placed with one of the leading firms in that field, Messrs Musgrave of Bolton.

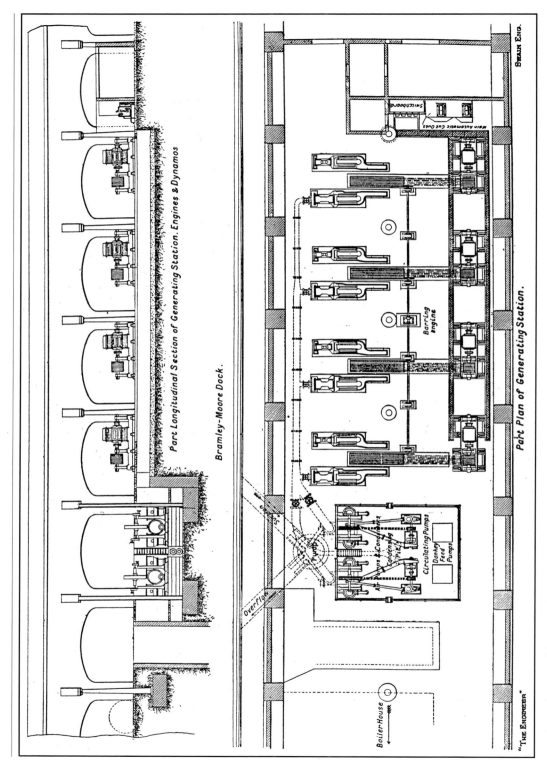

Part Longitudinal Section of Generating Station. Engines & Dynamos

Bramley-Moore Dock.

Part Plan of Generating Station.

Barring engine

Switchboard

Main Automatic Cut Outs

Swain Eng.

Air Pumps & Condensers

Condensate Tank

Circulating Pumps

Donkey Feed Pumps

Overflow

Boiler House

"The Engineer"

Part plan and section of the original arrangement of the enginehouse.

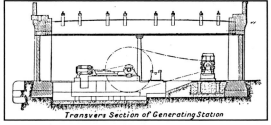

Transvers Section of Generating Station

Left: Transverse section of the enginehouse.

Below: Sections of the boilerhouse: notice the coal hopper for the automatic stokers shown in the transverse section.

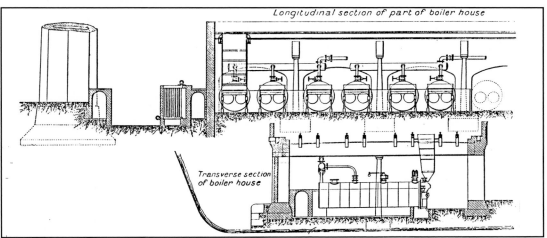

Longitudinal section of part of boiler house

Transverse section of boiler house

In one sense that may seem a stupid decision, in that the immediate future definitely lay with high-speed direct-coupled engines. Furthermore, one did not need to be clairvoyant to see that at the time. But there was more to it than that, for both the leading designs of high-speed engines suitable for direct coupling (Willans and Belliss & Morcom) had vertical cylinders and were thus comparatively lofty. In the confined space beneath the Coal Railway, horizontal mill engines had more to commend them than their tried-and-tested reliability and, as we shall see, the later addition of a Belliss-type engine was not an overwhelming success. It was not until 1927, when third-generation turbine-driven power stations of sizes and outputs unimaginable in 1893 were in service, that the LOR gave up the unequal struggle and closed down its generating station in favour of buying power from Liverpool City Council. This suggests that its original installation cannot have been as bad as it might seem at first sight.

The boilerhouse, at 98ft by 60ft, was quite large, and the original provision of six of the largest common size of Lancashire boilers (30ft by 8ft, and with Galloway-style cross-tubes) was generous. At the working pressure adopted, of 120lb/sq in, each of these boilers would be capable of handling one of the main engines on its own — and there were only four main engines. The man behind the electrical installation was Thomas Parker, and when he presented a paper to the Institution of Civil Engineers, he explained that owing to the lack of precedents from which to work, they had started by calculating the number of horsepower required to operate the trains and then added to that the appropriate figures for electrical and mechanical losses, thus arriving at a required engine power and, finally, a required evaporative capacity in the boilerhouse. When the line was extended, requiring more trains in motion at any one time, the engine power was increased by 50%, but the boiler power remained sufficient. Leaving aside the possibility of miscalculation or gross extravagance in the original provision of boiler capacity, this indicates an early intention either to extend the line or to increase the speed of the service.

It must be admitted that the boilerhouse was pretty primitive. Although equipped with effective automatic stokers and with Green's economisers to preheat the feed water, the waste heat from the boilerhouse was sufficient to cause the MD&HB to complain about damage to the track of the High Level Railway above. Since a good Cornish boilerhouse of 1840 could keep itself only minimally above ambient temperature, this could be taken as evidence of inefficiency bordering on downright crudity. Furthermore, although superheating was by then widely adopted as a means of effecting a fuel saving of up to 20% — and more in really

21

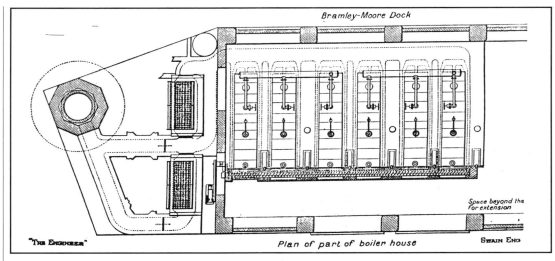

Bramley-Moore Dock

"The Engineer"   Plan of part of boiler house   Swain Eng

Space beyond this for extension

sophisticated installations — it was not adopted in the LOR generating station.

The enginehouse was a rather different matter. The engines were each capable of developing 400ihp at their normal working speed of 100rpm, and like most of their kind were capable of considerably more for short periods of acute need. Just as in mill practice, they used multiple rope drives (19 1.25in cotton ropes), and these were proportioned to give the 4.2:1 'gearing-up' ratio needed to achieve the right speed for the dynamos. As one would expect of Musgrave's, these were modern, efficient machines, using Corliss valvegear and quite a high expansion ratio, but compact they were not. Their flywheels, for example, were 14ft diameter and 3ft 2in wide. Allowing for a sufficient length of rope drive, they required a considerable width of enginehouse. The available space was, at 183ft by 60ft, more than adequate and was easily able to accommodate the later additions to the plant.

The engines had been so specified, as was normal, that three of the four could meet the anticipated maximum load (of 900ehp). The ability to maintain the service was pursued much further than that, though. An engineer's pocket book of the period reveals that the cotton ropes employed had a power-carrying capability 50ehp beyond 'normal practice'. That often troublesome unit, the condenser, was completely duplicated, as were the steam and feed pipes and their stop-valves. Each of the two boiler feed pumps could deliver 6,700gal/hr, which was sufficient for four boilers and thus easily sufficient for three engines. There was even a pipe which would allow the engines to exhaust direct to atmosphere should both condensers fail. This device proved its worth in 1894 by allowing the engines to keep running when the dock was drained for maintenance. The engines would, of course, run at reduced power

Above: Plan of the original extent of the boilerhouse, showing the six Lancashire boilers with their furnaces towards the bottom of the page. Between them and the chimney are the economisers; the solid black bars drawn in the flues are the flap valves for changing from one economiser to the other (as mentioned in the text).

and with an appalling fuel consumption, but clearly what mattered was that they would run and therefore the trains would not stop.

This was undoubtedly a wise policy. The public already loved complaining about the railways. The joke about the man who committed suicide by lying down on the railway line — 'poor devil died of starvation' — was current by 1880, as was the one about the invention of the sandwich-curling machine reputedly employed in station buffets. Nevertheless, the steam locomotive and its various support systems were tried, tested and generally reasonably reliable. To the Company, and perhaps more particularly to Thomas Parker, the consequences of something as unusual as an electric railway getting a reputation for unreliability would be extremely undesirable.

So the attention to detail went on. The dynamos themselves were electrically so robust that according to Parker they were capable, if all electrical control devices failed, of taking such an overload as to check the engines without damage to themselves. The normal output of each dynamo was 475A at 500V (dc) at 420rpm, corresponding to 300ehp. The engines each delivered 400ihp, which was a generous allowance for mechanical and transmission losses (which were actually of the order of 12%), making this capability of the dynamos the more remarkable. In achieving such a degree of 'unburstability' they reached the weight of 21.5 tons

each. They were also cunningly contrived to allow quite major maintenance, including removing the armatures, to be carried out without any disturbance to the engines or rope drives, which was just as well, given their cumbersome nature.

From the dynamos, the current passed to the main switchboard, which was an impressive structure of marble with ornamental polished wood framing and embellishments. There was an ammeter, a voltmeter and an overload cut-out (1,000A) for each dynamo, and from those the current passed to a 'bus bar and through a main 4,000A cut-out to the track. Originally there were just two mighty cables supplying the track at the nearest convenient point, but in 1896 feeder cables were added to help smooth out voltage variations along the route.

There were two later additions to the generating capacity. The first was rendered necessary by the Northern and Southern extensions, which involved up to eight extra traction motors on the line at peak times. The extra dynamos were basically similar to the originals and were supplied by Thomas Parker & Co Ltd of Wolverhampton. Although they were a little more sophisticated than their predecessors, they were made to similar overall dimensions so that in case of need the armatures were interchangeable. The extra engines were of the same configuration and output as the originals but were made by another famous Bolton builder, namely Hick, Hargreaves. They embodied a number of detail design improvements over the Musgrave engines, including a governor which was claimed to be much quicker and more sensitive in response to varying load conditions. They were built with an interesting cylinder block and valve chest which, instead of being a single extremely complicated casting, consisted of four much simpler castings bolted together. Although there is no positive record of it, these would almost certainly make maintenance much easier when the engines were getting older and required re-machining of cylinder bores or valve faces.

The last addition in terms of capacity resulted from the undertaking by the Company in 1900 to run a tram service to Crosby, and they now installed exactly the sort of 'modern' engine which their critics had suggested they should have installed at the outset. Messrs Browett & Lindley were licensed to build engines to Belliss and Morcom designs, and they provided what one would expect, namely a triple vertical tandem compound, fully enclosed and with a pressure lubrication system. It produced 1,500hp at 230rpm and had a British Schuckert dc multipolar generator direct-coupled to its crankshaft. The output of this machine was 1,650A at 500V, but it was clearly unsatisfactory as Box records that by 1909 it had been replaced by a 12-pole generator by Dick, Kerr of Preston which gave 1,700A at the same speed.

The installation of the Browett & Lindley engine allows us to judge whether the contemporary criticism by other engineers of the 'old-fashioned' mill engine installation was justified. To begin with, the new engine needed a hole dug in the floor for it, since it was too tall for the enginehouse. More to the point, it had a relatively low expansion ratio and hence an alarming hunger for steam. It is interesting to note in passing that in 1949, the Newcomen Society carried out an efficiency trial on what was then the oldest (at nearly 150 years) working engine in the country, a Watt beam engine in the Crofton pumping station of the Kennet & Avon Canal, and the figure they obtained of 29lb of steam/bhp/hr was about the same as the 'modern' Browett & Lindley engine achieved! Box, who remembered the generating station clearly from his youth, states that the Browett engine was eventually used only in emergency or on Sundays, when its output was sufficient to run the entire service on its own. On the other hand, it must be taken into account that one comparatively compact unit was producing more power than three of the original engines put together, with all the reduction in attendance and maintenance costs which that implied.

Above: The main switchboard in 1895.

Clearly a monster like that necessitated an increase in the steam supply, and Musgrave's gained the contract for supplying an extra Lancashire boiler, 9ft in diameter compared with the 8ft of the old ones, and with a superheater. Like the old boilers, it was served by a Vickers mechanical stoker, and like them it was force-fed a diet of extremely unpleasant Lancashire slack coal. The use of more steam meant the need for more condenser capacity, and an extra one was installed of sufficient size that it was still possible to keep one 'spare' in case of trouble.

This new addition increased the total generating capacity by about 50%, which seems excessive if all it was to do was drive a peak hour maximum of nine trams each with twin 25hp motors, a total of 450hp as against 1,500. As we shall see below, the Company had other ideas for using this surfeit of amps, in the shape of the 'Accelerated Service' on the railway.

At the same time that the Browett & Lindley engine was installed, an attempt at smoothing out the peaks and troughs in the load was made, in the form of two gargantuan batteries, reputedly the biggest in the country, each of 650A/hr capacity. The 'new' 1895 switchboard remained unaltered, a new and separate one serving to control the new generator and the rotary transformers which were used to transmit current at 1,100–1,150V to the tramway. This new board was, like the old ones, splendidly fashioned in marble and enhanced with fancy woodwork.

In 1900, Liverpool opened two large new municipal power stations of a little over 11MW each. By astute investment in tramways and street lighting, they managed to achieve a reasonably constant load around the clock, with the result that during the LOR's first decade the price of electricity in Liverpool roughly halved. The next wave of development in power station design came in the mid-1920s, coincident with the establishment of the national grid, by which time any half-decent power station was at least 20 times the size of the LOR's humble undertaking. In addition to being too small, obsolete and inefficient, the whole plant, especially the boilers, was getting a bit old, and one suspects that the uncertainties of coal supply brought about by the General Strike were a contributory factor in the Company's decision in 1927 to shut down the generating station as from 18 June and buy power from Liverpool Corporation. It saved a good deal of money, but as may be seen in Chapter 7, it needed to.

Chapter 3
Getting it Started

The refusal of the Dock Board to get directly involved in the building of the line resulted in the situation described at the end of Chapter 1, with a lease effectively placing Sir William Forwood in control of the rights both to form the company and to construct and operate the railway for which the Board had obtained powers in its earlier Acts of Parliament. Forwood was a remarkable man from a remarkable family. He was the son of Thomas Forwood, a Member of the Dock Board for 22 years, but he never served on the Board at all, throwing in his lot instead with the Chamber of Commerce, of which he was President from 1872–77. The Chamber commonly failed to see eye to eye with the Board, and it was not unknown for the two bodies to make public attacks on each other. He was a member of the Town (later City) Council for a total of 58 years, and Mayor or Lord Mayor in four of them. In the squabbles which pervaded Liverpool's commercial society he was firmly with the merchants against the shipowners, which tended to make him anti-Dock Board, since the Board was widely perceived as being dominated by shipowners. He was a man of such standing, however, that despite this, he was elected to the Board of the Cunard Steamship Company.

On the other hand he wholeheartedly subscribed to the Board's dislike and mistrust of mainline railway companies, a view he shared with both his father Thomas and his brother Arthur, so that the name of Forwood often occurs in evidence before inquiries or as a member of some Liverpool delegation complaining about railways. On one occasion he admitted that the reason the Chamber of Commerce had become the Incorporated Chamber of Commerce — an unusual and expensive move for a Chamber — was specifically to give it a locus standi for just such activities. He was, therefore, the right man for the Board in what appeared the critical areas. He would not sell out to a mainline company, he had the reputation for probity and the circle of associates which would help raise the money in difficult times, and he was a man of remarkable energy.

The lease did not directly empower Forwood to build the railway: for that he needed to establish the Company, which was duly done under an Act obtained in July 1888. He was to be the Chairman, and the rest of the Board was made up of merchants like himself. They already had the basis of the route, which ran from Alexandra Dock in the north to Herculaneum in the south, worked out — this was the route enabled by the Board's Act of 1888 — and the availability of the land was within the terms of the lease from the Board. The following year, the Company's prospectus was issued, seeking £450,000 in £10 shares. Shortly afterwards there occurs the first minor falling-out between Company and Board, for the Company, fearing that capital might not be easy to raise, tried to persuade the Board to buy 10,000 shares — nearly a quarter of the issue. The Board had not ducked the responsibility of building the railway just in order to put that sort of money into a venture they would not control, and on 1 November 1888 they firmly declined the suggestion. An outrageous piece of brinkmanship by Forwood — suggesting that the Company might get a contractor to take on construction for payment in shares to the value of £427,000 — soon changed their minds. They reluctantly agreed to buy the 10,000 shares if that made the difference between the project standing or falling. To everyone's surprise, money was readily forthcoming and the issue was over-subscribed, so that the Board ended up with only 5,000 shares. It is possible, of course, that the known support of the Board made the shares seem safer and more attractive to outsiders. If so, they were sadly misled.

Sir Douglas Fox and J. H. Greathead had been appointed consulting engineers for the project. Both were men of great distinction, but nearing the ends of their professional careers, so we may assume that theirs were primarily prestige names for the prospectus and that most of the work was done by the joint resident engineers (Sir) Francis Fox (younger brother of Sir Douglas) and S. B. Cottrell. Both these younger men already had impressive track records. Fox had worked on the Mersey Railway (and became a Director of the Company) and both had worked for the Manchester, Sheffield & Lincolnshire Railway, including the construction of what was then the largest swing bridge in the world, carrying that line across the River Dee at Hawarden. (This splendid structure is still in traffic, though unfortunately the end of shipping on the Dee allowed it to be fixed on its bearers some 15 years ago.) Fox went on to become a truly international figure, perhaps his personal turning point being his appointment to the Commission to advise on the

Simplon Tunnel project in 1894. Cottrell moved to the Wrexham, Mold & Connah's Quay Railway and then in 1892 became the first General Manager and Engineer of the Liverpool Overhead Railway Company.

These men had a somewhat unenviable task, in that the route they had come to build was not only not of their own choosing, but, as mentioned above and in Chapter 1, the subject of some pretty high-powered local politics. That they could not stay out of the politics is indicated by Cottrell getting sucked into the activities of the Chamber of Commerce as it investigated possible schemes for light railways designed to break the South Lancashire oligopoly enjoyed by the existing mainline companies. We need not look far to find who twisted his arm. There was one deviation from the original route, however, which was extremely desirable on engineering as well as political or financial grounds.

Most of the docks of Liverpool are reclaimed from the river. Although much of Herculaneum Dock was excavated from dry land, only Stanley Dock is entirely so, and stands on the inland side of the Dock Road. This was the only point at which the enabled route of the Overhead came into conflict with the movement of vessels. The original proposal had been to run the railway around three sides of Stanley Dock, for to have a movable bridge across the passage would effectively mean that ships could only leave or enter during the night. This proposal was most undesirable for the railway: it increased the overall length of the route by about 10% without offering any identifiable extra traffic. Worse than that, it had to cross the Dock Road twice and those bridges would have to be movable, as was the one carrying the High Level Coal Railway at Bramley, Moore Dock, to allow the passage of extraordinary loads on the Dock Road. Finally, it required four 90° bends, which would be difficult to accommodate in the existing street plan and the buildings lining those streets, without adopting unacceptably small radii.

A campaign of wheedling the Board to allow a route straight across Stanley passage was initially, and predictably, unsuccessful. In June 1890, however, the Board agreed to close Stanley passage during normal working hours on an experimental basis. In effect, they pretended that there was a railway bridge across it which could only be opened at night. Many reports later, they decided that the inconvenience was fairly slight, and in January 1891 they approved the proposed design for Stanley Bridge. It was an ingenious design by F. Hudleston, a staff engineer with the Contractor, which operated as a double-leaf swing bridge to clear the passage completely for a ship to pass, but also had twin bascules in the lower deck only, so that the fairly numerous small craft could be allowed through in the daytime without disturbing the railway.

Construction of the line had begun in November 1889, with J. W. Willans of Manchester as Principal Contractor. He, in fact, sub-contracted most of the work, but retained the fairly critical task of planting the main structure in the ground. Along much of the route the local red sandstone was near enough to the surface that the cheapest method was to pile down to it and stand the columns on the piles, but where it lay deeper, concrete foundation blocks were used. Because the loads varied in different places, so did the blocks, and their sizes were calculated to keep the loads to below 1 ton per sq ft. Put like that, in engineer-speak, it sounds easy. In real life it was not: exactly the problem the railway was intended to solve saw to that. Where, on a road/railway that was filled beyond capacity, did you pile up spoil or store materials? As in most ports, pilferage was endemic: where did you keep your tools? Long and tedious was the correspondence with the Dock Board for securing the temporary use of small parcels of land. The Board was not only in receipt of the piteous whinings of the Company and its contractor for working space, but also of the purple-faced outpourings of merchants and shipowners whose frenetic comings and goings were delayed.

In the main, the Board was amazingly helpful and tolerant. Temporary closures of gateways, the loan of small patches of ground for spoil- or stock-heaps and even occasional small gifts of materials from the dockyard stores were readily forthcoming. Most remarkable of all, it allowed the erection of huts. The Board was paranoiac about huts, because it knew from long and bitter experience that temporary huts became permanent and permanent huts did dirty things together when no one was looking, and proliferated. Major shipping companies were peremptorily instructed to remove huts, so the Company's being allowed to erect them indicates a quite unusual degree of helpfulness.

Needless to say, the Contractor found a few nasty surprises lying in wait below ground, but considering the route — right through the shoreline of 'Olde' Liverpool — matters were not too bad. There was a stretch of old sewer which had, in effect, to be bridged over because it ran along, rather than across, the route. They ran into the retaining wall of the entrance to the Old Dock (closed in 1826), which they could perfectly easily have avoided had they employed a Port Historian like the present author on their team. They found some old wooden waterpipes, dating from before the times of municipal supply, but then so does everybody who digs a few feet deep round there. Overall, the provision of foundations was fairly painless.

The next step was relatively easy as well. The columns were made up of two channels and two strips riveted into a box section. These sat grouted in a cast-iron socket secured to the foundations, and

Above: Seaforth Sands station in its early days. *IAL*

Below: Seaforth Sands from the track: notice the ladders and the fact that the insulators on the conductor rails are shiny bright. This just might be a pre-opening shot. *IAL*

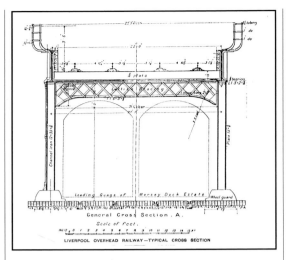

General Cross Section. A.

Scale of foot.

LIVERPOOL OVERHEAD RAILWAY—TYPICAL CROSS SECTION

Left: General arrangement of the normal form of columns, girders and bracing.

appointed place and erected. The standard span was chosen as 50ft, but the various constraints at and below ground level meant that a few abnormal spans would be needed. In the event, 'a few' turned out to be two-thirds of the total length. Some spans were more abnormal than others. The 'normal' arrangement was that two main girders, 4ft deep with 16in flanges, rested on the columns with the decking resting on the lower flanges. At each pair of columns was a light lattice beam to enhance the lateral stiffness. Sadly, there were places where columns and girders would not readily coincide, requiring the use of shelf brackets larger than one can buy in B&Q, so cross-beams between the columns and below the main girders were interpolated.

Shortening a standard span was easy, but lengthening one gave rise to uneasy thoughts of sagging in the middle, so the main girders of overlength spans were made deeper. The comfortable picture of standardisation recedes further: not only did the actual lengths of span vary from 30ft to 75ft, but there were three major roads close to the Pier Head where even overlength spans would not reach and bowstring girder bridges of 98ft span had to be constructed. One standard feature did remain: the spans were wide enough to accommodate the curves, so spans were constructed straight, forming curves as a series of tangents (or chords, depending on which way you looked at it) with wedge-shaped bits that might reasonably be termed 'bodging pieces' in between.

These fairly numerous breaches of standardisation were what remained after a good deal of alteration at ground level. Various police huts and other minor buildings were removed, as were two more substantial customs depots. In many places, the columns had to be set into the boundary wall of the Dock Estate, and the remains of a couple of dozen of these may still be seen at the time of writing.

There were two major difficulties, both connected with other railways. The first was the High Level Coal Railway, which ran from the Lancashire & Yorkshire yard at Sandhills, crossing the Dock Road and railway to join a T-shaped viaduct which ran along the east sides of Wellington and Bramley-Moore Docks and the north side of Bramley-Moore.

were protected with a large cast-iron 'bumper' filled with concrete. Such protection was very necessary, since the distinctive Liverpool team wagons had large iron-armoured wheel naves: the gross weight of the wagons could exceed 10 tons and they were drawn by two heavy horses in tandem, weighing another 2–2.5 tons. Things they bumped tended to stay bumped, so it was important to prevent their getting at the columns.

The difficult part of the job was above the tops of the columns. The confined working spaces along the route made it highly desirable to assemble the main members in a central works yard, so the idea was hatched of using a standard length of span between columns. These standard spans could then be constructed in the yard, trundled off to their

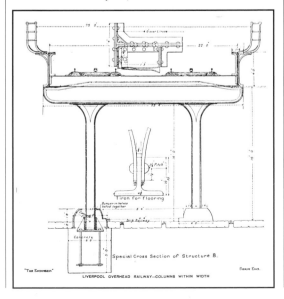

Special Cross Section of Structure B.

"The Engineer"   Swain Eng.

LIVERPOOL OVERHEAD RAILWAY—COLUMNS WITHIN WIDTH

Left: General arrangement of the commonest alternative form, used where the columns could not be spaced to suit the main girders.

Above: This view across St Nicholas' Place was probably taken on the same day as the two shots in Chapter 1. The immense width of the 'Pier Head Approaches' required two overlength spans and a bowstring bridge.

Its height, which related to the height necessary for bunkering ships or loading cargo coal at the time it was designed in 1852, was very close to that intended for the Overhead. Because wagons were lifted and tipped singly, they were handled singly by horses and hydraulic capstans. There were two lines of track which handled, on average, a couple of hundred wagons each way per day. Since most of these wagons moved singly, the number of 'train movements' was high. A level crossing with an electric railway running about a 5min service each way was unlikely to meet with the approval of the Board of Trade. The Overhead had, therefore, to descend to ground level and climb back again to its normal height in a section which became known to LOR staff as 'The Switchback' — the old name for what we now call a roller-coaster. This did not employ 'standard' spans, but was constructed of masonry with rusticated red sandstone facing.

Because Hartley was a parsimonious Yorkshireman, and had envisaged the Dock Line of Railway as worked by horses, he had not incurred any

superfluous expense in so aligning the route as to make it usable by anything larger than a 10-ton wagon. (Before accusations of regional stereotyping are made, it may be pointed out that only Leeds has the gall to designate as 'The Square' something which has only three sides.) If the Overhead was to follow over the top of his route, then to maintain clearances on both levels, either the structure would have to be superfluously wide or the lines below would need quite extensive realignment. This led to considerable ill-feeling between the Board and the Company. The arrangement mentioned above whereby Lyster's department was authorised 'to supply any small amounts of material which might be needed' was interpreted by the Company to include all the materials needed for substantial alteration to the dock railway. This was, of course, refused as being completely beyond the intentions of the Board. Claims for 'betterment' dragged on for years, though it is interesting that the most significant 'betterment' — that at Queens Dock — was never mentioned.

Although nearly all the cargo passing through the docks came in assorted packages which did not exceed 5ft in any dimension, there were export cargoes like railway locomotives or marine boilers which came in large indivisible lumps. The numerous graving docks (dry docks) were not only used for scraping and painting hulls, but also for

Left: View down Chapel Street, with the St Nicholas' Place bridge. *IAL*

Left: Looking up James Street from Mann Island, probably early 1920s, judging by the petrol dustcart and the Bellamy trams in the distance. *IAL*

Below: The Brunswick bascule bridge being lifted... *IAL*

major repairs and alterations, with the result that such items as boilers might need to be delivered to them. It was, in short, not acceptable for the Overhead to form an unbroken barrier from end to end. At Brunswick, Sandon and Langton Docks, hydraulically-operated single-leaf bascule bridges were provided to allow extraordinary loads to pass through at night. Each of these was close both to graving docks and to heavy-lift quayside cranes.

We have made a notional journey around the meeting rooms and drawing boards and found the solutions to all the problems — except for the two biggest ones. These were making the structure stiff enough to withstand the acceleration, braking and centrifugal forces, and finding a way of erecting the spans without getting lynched by carters. G. A. Hobson, staff engineer with Willans, devised the ingenious arrangement whereby the decking surface supplied a considerable part of the strength. One of the features of the New York elevated railway which was thought unsuitable for copying in Liverpool was the way it allowed oil, water, ash and cinders to fall on anyone foolish enough to venture below, which resulted in the requirement in the Overhead Railway Act for a waterproof decking. (This was, of course, the origin of the railway's nickname of 'The Dockers' Umberella' [sic].)

Hobson's decking consisted of $\frac{5}{16}$in plates, normally 22ft long, bent longitudinally and riveted to T-bars, as shown in the diagram. The bending was done hot with dies under a hydraulic press, and a few teething troubles were encountered and overcome. Work improved with practice, so that by the end of the job,

Above: ...and fully open. *IAL*

Below: This fanciful view of the Dock Road is inaccurate in almost every possible respect apart from its reasonably authentic representation of the meeting of the LOR with the L&YR. Particularly endearing are the columns at the mid-point of the lifting span of the High Level bridge! The sailing ship is standing in the Huskisson Goods Depot.

General arrangement of the Hobson decking, with details of rivet spacings etc.

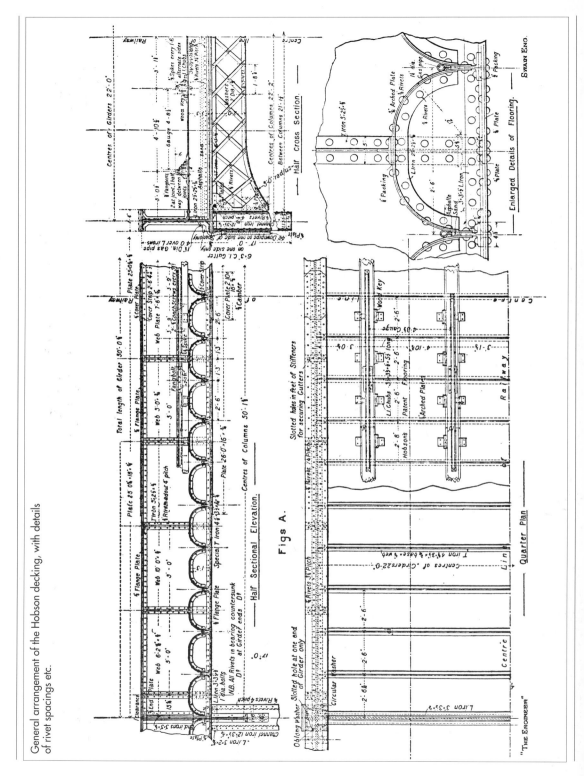

Half Cross Section.

Enlarged Details of Flooring.

SWAIN ENG.

Half Sectional Elevation.

Figs A.

Quarter Plan

Above: The curves to the north of Alexandra were not part of the passenger route to begin with, but the centrifugal forces they generated can well be imagined.

one gang of men could produce 64 plates ready for riveting in a day. An ingenious special-purpose riveter was used which kept pace with the production of the plates. This flooring was found to be extremely strong for its weight: in particular it was very stiff laterally, to resist centrifugal forces on the curves. Various sections of it were tested, and while the overall figures are pretty tedious, it may be worth remarking that a section 7ft 6in long (and 22ft wide) required 163 tons to cause total failure. A typical 50ft span weighed only 22 tons.

This operation of making up the decking was undertaken at a works yard between the original northern terminus and the carriage sheds, on the site which later became the LMS North Mersey Goods Depot. The main girders and other components were delivered to the yard, and nearly all of the spans were made up there, prior to meeting the final problem: erecting the structure with the minimum of obstruction to traffic at ground level. The contractor came up with a most ingenious solution, which was to work from one end to the other, using the portion which was built to transport the next span to its place and position it for fastening. Once the first span was up, the two outermost rails were laid (which was a gauge of 16ft) and a purpose-built trolley was placed on them. The next span to be erected was placed on the trolley,

timbered up to clear the tops of the main girders of the span(s) it was running on, and moved to the end, where it met the 'erecting apparatus'. This strange device, shown in the illustration, stood on long legs on the dock railway at its leading end and on wheels on the main girders of the last span erected. On its top were two gantry cranes, so that it could pick up a span from the trolley, and then be drawn forward until the span could be lowered onto the columns. It was possible to erect over 600ft per week by this method with absolutely minimal obstruction below. The complaints about obstruction received by the Board nearly all related to places like Bramley-Moore where the erecting apparatus could not be used. One cannot help but feel, however, that the Board itself must have shown some forbearance with respect to the occupation of its lines by the erecting span.

Once the structure was up, the track was laid very cheaply and simply. On the tops of the arches of the Hobson decking were riveted iron lugs which held down longitudinal sleepers, and super-elevation on curves was achieved by the equally simple method of making the sleepers thicker on one side than on the other. The track was ordinary flat-bottomed steel of only 56lb/yd, spiked and fang-bolted to the sleepers. There were no special difficulties in the tracklaying apart from the need to guard against earth leakage (from the return current in the running rails) finding its way into the structure via a fang-bolt and thus effecting an illicit liaison with one of the spikes which secured the sleepers. This arrangement, like the Hobson decking , was light, cheap and effective, but would eventually prove sadly lacking in durability.

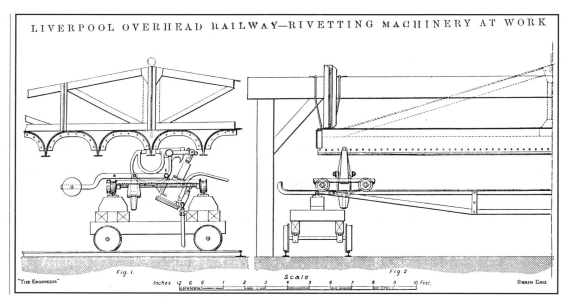

LIVERPOOL OVERHEAD RAILWAY—RIVETTING MACHINERY AT WORK

Fig. 1.

Fig 2

Scale

Inches 12 6 0 1 2 3 4 5 6 7 8 9 10 Feet

"The Engineer"

Swain Eng.

THE ENGINEER

Above left: The ingenious special-purpose riveting machine used for assembling the decking.

Left: A rather more artistic version of the riveting machine.

Above: The portable air compressor for supplying the riveters, both in the yard and along the route as construction advanced. The boiler is on the right and the air receiver on the left.

Right: Possibly the world's oddest steam locomotive, specially built when the distance to be travelled by the trolley became excessive for horse haulage from below.

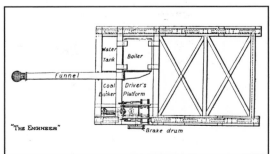

"THE ENGINEER"

Left: The temporary workshops below the old Seaforth Sands station. There seems to be no shortage of work for the wheel lathe. *IAL*

Below left: A similar view taken in the opposite direction. Both were dated by Box to 1924. *IAL*

Right: Same location, different view, showing the machining bay. None of the machines visible and identifiable looks as though it was necessarily new in 1893. *IAL*

Below: This view from the old station shows the carriage shed, with the original workshops underneath, in the background. It had to go to make way for the completion of Gladstone Dock. *IAL*

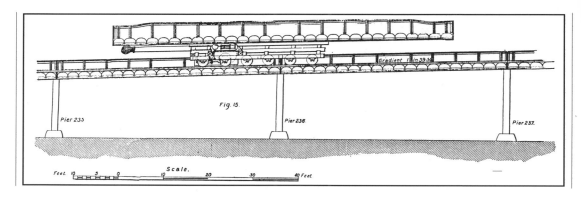

Fig. 15.

Pier 235. Pier 236. Pier 237.

Gradient 1 in 39.34

Feet. 10   5   0   10   20   30   40 Feet.

Scale.

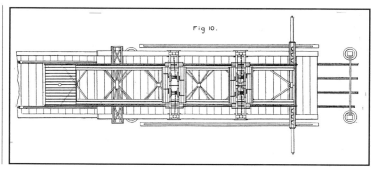

Fig 10.

Top: The trolley connected to the special locomotive. Horizontal chimneys never caught on, but the draught of this one was said to be adequate.

Above: General view of the erecting span (or 'gauntry') in action. In the background is the gantry of the works yard which delivered spans to the trolley.

Left & right: Plan (left), elevation and sections (right) of the erecting span.

Above: End view of the erecting span in the process of lowering a section of the structure into position. The gentlemen below obviously have confidence in the equipment.

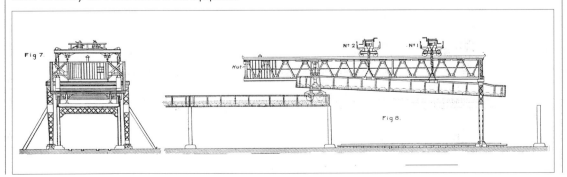

Above: Gladstone Dock station was the only one with overbridges. This view looks northwards, showing the bowstring bridge over Fort Road in the background... *IAL*

Below: ...and this one looks west, showing the new three-storey transit sheds of Gladstone No 1 Branch in the background, and the unmistakable jib of the Mammoth floating crane... *IAL*

The first official trial trip on the railway took place on 7 January 1893, when the Chairman received a party of engineers and Fairly Important People who were taken to each terminus and then for a tour of the generating station. This trip proved that everything worked correctly (although the final inspection by the Board of Trade was yet to be completed), so arrangements for the official opening could begin. Although the railway was under six miles long, it was widely recognised as being potentially epoch-making, which explains why the ceremonial starting of the generating engines was effected by no less a personage than the Prime Minister, Lord Salisbury, on 4 February. The distinguished group of guests included such luminaries as Lord Kelvin and much was made of the future potential of electrical technology, including the demonstration of a telephone connection to the House of Commons. The hacks of the local press were amused by the fact that the speakers who followed Lord Salisbury in the proceedings had to make themselves heard above the sound of the machinery, though there would need to be something pretty badly wrong with a Musgrave installation for it to inconvenience any except those who really were unaccustomed to public speaking. There followed the inevitable trip on a specially decorated train, and dinner as guests of the Lord Mayor, Richard Holt. In these days of impoverished local government and the Central Purchasing Department Sausage Roll it is perhaps necessary to recall that in the 1890s different rules applied and such functions were not only of some magnificence but were also presented with a style often lacking in students of the community catering college.

The original route ran from Alexandra Dock to Herculaneum Dock. Alexandra was by far the largest dock in the Liverpool system, consisting of a main or 'spine' dock of nearly 18 acres, from which extended three branch docks totalling about another 20 acres. Because it had deeper water than the older docks (though not really deep enough to cater for the continuing growth of the ships which sought to use it) and very generous quayside space, it attracted an enormous trade from the outset. Within a couple of years of opening it was handling over a fifth of the total tonnage of the port, mostly in the highly profitable North American trades. On any reasonably busy day, up to a dozen large ships, of perhaps 4,000

tons, were to be found loading or discharging in a frenzy of activity involving well over 100 men per ship. Less visible from the train windows was the small army of people weighing, counting and sampling goods, but aboard the trains there were often groups of them travelling to the next consignment which needed their attention.

The station at Alexandra was extremely basic. The initial proposal had been to construct island platforms, thus doing away with the need for overbridges and requiring only one staircase up from street level. This was 'found to be impractical'. That is to say, someone realised that whenever trains crossed at a station, which they were bound to do from time to time, the result would be not merely chaotic but probably dangerous. Twin platforms with separate staircases which rose from a ticket office, were built instead. Passengers leaving the station did so via a one-way turnstile. The platform buildings were entirely of timber and consisted only of a 'waiting-shed' with a small awning on each side. This was virtually a standard station design, the only exceptions being at Pier Head, Canning and Herculaneum. They formed a worthy development of the parsimonious ideas of Alfred Holt, but were still a considerable improvement on what had gone before.

Alexandra Dock was the beginning of the journey, but not the beginning of the line. The railway extended more than half a mile further to the north, passing by Hornby, the northernmost dock, and over the North Mersey Goods Yard where the Overhead's structure was built, to the carriage sheds and workshops. Here the track opened out to five roads, providing space for spare stock and also for minor maintenance and bodywork repairs. Down below, at ground level, were the workshops for more serious mechanical and electrical work, served by a hoist which lowered a complete truck for attention. This seemingly extravagant extra length of track was made necessary by lack of available land below at any more convenient point, but it was in any case a racing certainty that the Dock Estate would eventually extend further northwards, and thus provide a traffic for the 'superfluous' length leading to the sheds. The north entrances to the docks were already being outgrown, and the traffic density was mounting: while Forwood may not have foreseen exactly what would be built, he was certainly bright

enough to recognise that something like the Gladstone Dock system would eventually arrive to put new money in the company coffers.

The line south from Alexandra was straight as far as the next station, Brocklebank Dock, which was all of 696yd. About halfway along that stretch trains passed the Langton Graving Docks, with their amazing pumping station built in the style of a Bavarian fairy-tale castle and their equally amazing 100-ton hydraulic crane, designed to serve both vessels under repair and vessels loading indivisible heavy cargoes. This was another very busy place; this time busy with tradesmen and their labourers engaged in scaling and painting vessels, carrying out plating repairs below the waterline and attending to rudders and stern tubes. So busy did Langton eventually become that it had its own station from 1896–1906, only 300yd out of Alexandra. Over beyond Langton Dock the river entrances at Canada Basin were visible. They were depicted on the Overhead Railway Company's advertising posters, but seen in the flesh they looked very different. The poster designer evidently disapproved of Jesse Hartley's somewhat eccentric hydraulic pumping station, and left it out. (For which his artist's licence should have been endorsed.) Passengers on the railway could see it in all its perverse glory, an enormous stone building quite as crazy as Lyster's pumping station at the graving docks, except that this one was in medieval style, with a ponderous

castellated tower to house the hydraulic accumulators.

This entrance basin, with its locks, was originally opened in 1859, when both were of very ample size for the largest ships in the world. Despite modernisation in 1876 and 1890, it was still somewhat shallow for the largest ships of 1893, but the vessels of famous passenger lines like Cunard and White Star still came in there to discharge and load their cargoes and stores, carry out any minor repairs and take on board contract gangs of shore-based ship cleaners. These, together with the hundreds of crew who had an opportunity for some shopping or a night on the town, formed another part of the customer-base of the railway. In the first class compartments, ships' officers travelled to and from the city centre stations for business and pleasure alike.

Leaving Brocklebank station, the line curved for the first time in the course of the 1,068yd to Canada Dock. This dock was intended for the large paddle steamers used for passenger and packet trades, mainly on the North Atlantic, but with the construction of newer docks to the north, Canada passed largely into the hands of the timber trade, most of which was still carried on by the traditional method, with sailing ships which discharged through bow-ports, and moored stem-on to the quay. Every available bit of quay space was stacked full of timber. The fire hazard was considerable, with steam-driven overhead gantry cranes — shunned on safety grounds in many parts of the Dock Estate — in use for stacking the butts. The danger was no illusion, for on 5 August 1893, four timber yards were destroyed by fire, the estimated value of the loss being £100,000. The heat from the fire damaged the sleepers of the Overhead but did not do any serious harm to the structure.

The line continued straight again for the 717yd to Sandon Dock, where there was another concentration of graving docks. Along this stretch, the VIPs at the opening would have their first real encounter with some of the larger-scale activities of the Dock Engineer. At Canada, the construction of a branch dock was well under way, together with some enlargement of the dock itself; the two improvements together would add nearly 14 acres of water area to the system.

Away on the far side of Huskisson Dock, a pumphouse with a lofty chimney would be seen making some smoke: its job was to raise the water level in the docks artificially, and it was part of the same scheme to deepen and modernise these obsolescent docks to enable them to accommodate some of the vast new ships which were on the drawing boards, like Cunard's *Campania* and *Lucania.* These were not really large-scale works, so there were only about a thousand men on site, but in addition to their comings and goings the railway benefited from innumerable site meetings between suppliers and contractors with the junior members of the Dock Engineer's staff who travelled from their office at Coburg Dockyard. Some of them travelled first class.

In the first year of the railway's operation, there was an extraordinary row between Lyster and the General Manager and Secretary — Miles Kirk Burton — over the purchase of books of prepaid first class tickets for use by Lyster's staff. This ended with a complete prohibition on the purchase of first class tickets for staff use. Given that engineers were meant to look like and behave like gentlemen, it seems a little hard to have expected them to share third class accommodation with their contractors' labourers, but such was the case.

As part of the changing pattern of trade which was brought about by the changes to this group of docks, Sandon station was closed in 1896 and replaced by Huskisson some 160yd to the north and Nelson, 623yd to the south. Huskisson Dock became the base for the Cunard and Ellerman lines, while Nelson long remained what was known in the

Harbourmaster's Department as a 'pet dock', one which was particularly popular with the customers. Despite the fact that it dated from 1848, it was much in demand for the largest classes of coaster and continued to handle enough of them to amount to a very large total tonnage. Since the cargo-handling techniques in obsolescent docks were pretty rudimentary, the numbers of men, and hence potential customers for the railway, were large, even before we allow for the fact that lots of smallish ships carrying lots of smallish consignments generated huge amounts of paperwork, and hence plenty of paperworkers travelling to and fro.

Between Nelson and Clarence the line passed under the High Level Coal Railway by 'The Switchback' described in Chapter 3. In the process, passengers travelled alongside the coal railway on its robust brick arches at Wellington and Bramley-Moore Docks. There was a fancy accumulator tower, and under part of the tracks lay a hydraulic pumping station which provided the power for the wagon cranes and the capstans used to move the wagons around. There was another chimney here as well: it belonged to the Overhead Railway generating station. Climbing sharply on its masonry-faced incline, the railway regained its aerial view and passengers could see that the coal railway by then mainly supplied coal into barges and floating elevators. Ocean-going ships had mostly got either too deep to get into the dock alongside, or too lofty to get under the coaling cranes.

Soon after the track regained 'standard height' it reached the double-decker swing bridge at Stanley Dock. Here was the oldest of the hydraulic pumping stations of the Dock Estate, built in 1855 and again possessed of a castellated accumulator tower, complete with arrow-slits. Passing over the bridge, there was a good view of the roughly square Stanley Dock, with its warehouses either side, and at the far end a mousehole of a bridge. This carried Great Howard Street (named after the prison reformer who influenced the design of the 'new' Liverpool gaol a bit further on) over the Leeds & Liverpool Canal. Like the other 'warehouse docks', Stanley was a very labour-intensive place: hundreds were employed in the warehouses; not just in handling goods but in repairing casks, sampling the moisture content of tobacco and performing all the innumerable tasks necessary to prevent people diddling HM Customs & Excise. By the time the railway was built, the dock was already obsolescent, so that the warehouses did more business by road, rail and canal than they did by ship. That definitely did not mean that they were unprofitable to the Dock Board, and neither did it reduce the numbers of railway customers coming and going. The Dock Road was still carried over Stanley Passage by one of the old double-leaf cast-iron swing bridges which

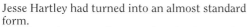

Jesse Hartley had turned into an almost standard form.

To the right was Collingwood Dock, the last dock on the estate to be purpose-built for coasting traffic, and beyond it lay Salisbury, a half-tide dock with a triple river entrance. On the island between the two main entrance passages stood the Salisbury clock, a spectacular hexagonal tower which seemed, indeed still seems, at first sight, to be merely the means for supporting a large clock which, having six faces, can be seen from all points of the compass. It has been unkindly suggested that its real purpose was to display Jesse Hartley's ego to all points. In fact, the tower fulfilled a number of useful functions for the Harbourmaster's department, including the provision of a vantage point for observing approaching traffic and the mounting of a large signal bell for issuing instructions. Although these docks were, by 1893, no longer in the front line of the major traffics, the entrance remained a very busy one, serving a large number of coastal and short-sea users.

Clarence Dock station provided the perceptive passenger with a couple of astonishing insights into how the docks really worked. First were the two graving docks with their entry basin: opened in 1830

they were comprehensively obsolete, yet still very much in demand for any vessels small enough to be able to use them. (They were extensively modernised in 1929–30, and are in use to this day.) Clarence Dock itself had seen virtually no modernisation since it was opened as a specialist steam dock, also in 1830, yet its paltry 10 acres — including its half-tide basin — were thronged with vessels varying between the inconsequential and the negligible. So many of these humble craft were coming and going so quickly in the 1890s that in tonnage terms it was the fourth-rated dock in the system, and it carried more than the 160 acres of the entire Birkenhead system. The result of all this activity was, of course, that a very minor dock had one of the more popular stations on the railway.

Leaving Clarence Dock, the railway passed Trafalgar and Victoria Docks, which were nearly as decrepit as Clarence. Waterloo, the next dock southwards was, like them, opened in the 1830s, but had been extensively modernised to provide specialist bulk grain berths, and the warehouses towered over the railway. They employed comparatively little labour, for they were highly mechanised. The buyers and sellers with their samples had a longish walk, by Overhead standards,

Far left: Virtually identical with the one at Brunswick, but this is the Sandon bascule bridge. Something at its tail end is obviously causing concern. *IAL*

Left: This must also be the one at Sandon: the Coburg Granary is not visible. The mystery is what has happened to the conductor rails. If it were a 'demolition shot' the running rails would be rusty. *IAL*

Above right: The view northwards from near the foot of 'The Switchback', with the High Level Coal Railway passing over the LOR. *IAL*

Right: A northbound train leaving Clarence Dock station in the latter days of the railway, conceivably even a post-closure stock movement, as the signal is showing no light. *IAL*

for there was no station at Waterloo and the gap between Clarence and Princes, 1,026yd, was the third longest on the entire route. Furthermore, West Waterloo was a very busy general-purpose dock, often occupied by large sailing ships which presumably offered plenty of potential traffic to the Overhead.

Between Waterloo and Princes lay Princes Half-Tide, a squarish basin with a triple entrance not unlike that at Salisbury. By the time the Overhead was built it was primarily concerned with transferring small cargoes to Mersey 'Flats' (the local sailing barges) and so only offered a relatively small railway traffic, mainly in clerks and messengers.

Princes was another 'pet dock'. Opened in 1821, it was large but rather shallow, and its walls still had a pronounced 'batter' which made life difficult for modern steamships with their relatively square midship section and protruding bilge keels, but it retained the vital advantage of being close to the commercial action. Despite its age and general awkwardness, it still ranked third in the port for tonnage shifted, handling a mixture of trades from far-flung places like Latin America and rather nearer-flung ones like Belfast. Like almost every dock the railway passed south of Huskisson, it was a

remnant of once-proud trades which still somehow contrived to make a useful living. The transit sheds on the east side were still the 'Hartley Pattern' ones like those at Clarence, but they would not remain much longer, for in 1894 a fire destroyed one-third of their length — and the ship tied up alongside at the time. Even so, the complete modernisation of the East Princes sheds would have to wait until the proceeds of selling Clarence Dock to the Corporation to infill for the site of their new power station became available — in 1928.

As the Overhead approached Princes Dock station, it crossed over the line from the LNWR Waterloo Goods Depot, which arrived at the edge of the Dock Estate from Edge Hill via two tunnels and a cutting. This connection was not very important in 1893, but would soon become so, for the somnolent port of Southampton passed into railway company control. Heavy investment soon turned it into a serious competitor in the North Atlantic passenger trade. The Dock Board's response was the construction of Riverside station, opened in 1896, which allowed mainline trains access to a station within 50yd of the ship's side. For those unimportant persons who did not have first class through tickets from London to New York, the LOR Princes Dock station might well

Left: A view of the double-deck swing bridge at Stanley, looking south, with the south leaf swung 'off'. The old double-leaf road swing bridge is to the left. *IAL*

Left: This view of one leaf of the Stanley Bridge shows clearly how the bascule section lifted for small craft. *IAL*

Below: There seem to be dozens of photographs of this event: Stanley Bridge loaded up with LOR trains and MD&HB locomotives for a proof test. This cannot have been the original test, as MD&HB did not own any locomotives until 1904. *IAL*

prove useful. A large liner of 1893 carried about 500 second and third class passengers and about 400 crew, nearly all of whom were potential LOR customers. As the size of liners rocketed, so did the corresponding numbers: Mauretania (1907) carried 464 second and 1,138 third class passengers and a crew of 812.

There was another, less glamorous, side to the railway's traffic at Princes Dock, for although the floating stage was only enabled to take the giant passenger liners a couple of years after the railway opened, it was already the longest floating stage in the world, and home not only to 10 river ferry services, but to short sea ferries to Ireland, the Isle of Man, North Wales and a few other places. Many hundreds of visits per year were made by other coastwise passenger steamers. There was also extensive 'lightering' of passengers: in 1890, for example, 1,828 calls at the stage were made by tenders serving passenger liners anchored in the river.

From Princes, the route continued virtually straight to Pier Head station, a distance of 792yd. A number of engineering problems were surmounted in this short section, including the need to build columns into the old boundary wall, and at one point to realign the wall quite drastically. There are also two very wide streets, requiring the use of two of the four bowstring girder bridges on the route to cross them: respectively, St Nicholas' Place and the bottom of Water Street, immediately before which was the station. The reader will be familiar with the scene there today, with the famous trio of the Dock Offices, Cunard Building and Liver Building. When the railway opened, this huge reservoir of potential custom still lay in the future, for George's Dock, opened in 1777 and completely obsolete, was still there. Little traffic used it: photographs of its lingering death show a few fruit schooners, Mersey flats and assorted semi-derelict sailing vessels which look as though they could well be under arrest and awaiting sale for non-payment of dues. Not until 1900 was this little time-capsule infilled, providing the site for what everyone now thinks of as the Liverpool waterfront. On the other side of the track, running roughly along what is now the middle of the Dock Road, stood the Goree Warehouses, a tall arcaded structure built to replace the warehouses destroyed in the famous fire of 1802. The 'new' warehouses were heavily damaged during the May Blitz and mostly demolished shortly after peace broke out, though a small portion at the north end outlived the railway.

Pier Head was one of two *de luxe* stations. Not only did it have awnings extending beyond the platform edges, it even had two staircases each side, reflecting the expectation from the start that it would be much busier than the average station. The expectation was right to begin with, for so many people wanted to get from the relatively distant docks to the city centre for business or pleasure. The growth of huge shipping offices in the immediate vicinity continued into the 1930s, providing a steady dribble of potential new passengers, and Pier Head was also the station for 'Change (the Cotton Exchange), the main banking and insurance area of town and the Mersey Ferries.

Such was the density of business that stations now came thick and fast: over a third bowstring bridge and beside some more quaint remnants of rising a century ago at Mann Island, lay James Street station, only 330yd from Pier Head. For those wanting to buy fishing nets, ladders or rigging materials, this was the place to alight, but James Street itself was handily placed for large numbers of shipping offices and agencies great and small, as well as the Corn Exchange. It was also the place to alight to visit the Harbourmaster's Office or if you wanted to go to Birkenhead and preferred suffocation to contracting *mal-de-mer*(sey) on the ferries, for the Mersey Railway, still steam-hauled and repellent in the extreme, had its station just across the road. Finally, we should remember that the floating stage was so long that it straddled three stations. James Street was the most convenient for its upstream end.

The track continued with its legs buried in the boundary wall past Canning Dock to Custom House station, just 274yd from James Street, and the second of the *de luxe* models. Here were throngs of small shipping-related businesses — provisioners, chandlers, engineer's merchants, medicine chest suppliers, but above all business was generated by the Custom House itself and by the Dock Offices which were, until 1907, partly in rented space within the Custom House. The Traffic Office was across the road, at Albert Dock. Just inland of the Custom House stood the Sailors' Home, a charitable institution designed to provide sailors with the means of escape from 'land-rats' and extortionists. It was symbolic that it stood near the bottom of that same Paradise Street which features in 'Blow the man down'. Those who sought the protection of the Sailors' Home and those who thought nice girls loved sailors and found that only nasty ones did, were alike in being potential customers for the Overhead.

The railway did nothing very exciting before arriving at Wapping Dock station, 808yd further on. The line passed Albert and Salthouse Docks, now past their prime and dealing mainly in coasting trade, but at Albert as at Wapping there were large bonded warehouses involving much coming and going both of employees and of those buying and selling. In between lay Kings Dock, little improved in the century since it was built, and due for a reconstruction which would quite soon render it

unrecognisable. Wapping was also the site of a vast LNWR depot on the inland side of the Dock Road — the site of the original Liverpool & Manchester Railway's arrival at the docks. Along the side streets which climb from the Dock Road rose a hotch-potch of warehousing, some specialising in particular commodities, some general. Every one generated comings and goings at the station.

Brunswick Dock station was another 742yd, in the space of which the contentious section at East Queens, mentioned above, was passed. Like so many of the docks in the middle stretch of the railway, Brunswick and Queens were overdue for major modernisation, and the first step had already been taken, in the shape of installing impounding pumps to provide an artificial improvement in depth. It would take until 1908 for the entire programme to reach completion and turn Brunswick, Coburg, Queens, Wapping and Kings into thoroughly serviceable modern docks. Brunswick station was, however, important because it was the one which served the MD&HB Engineer's Depot, known as the Dock Yard. The Engineer-in-Chief had his office there, and his department spent about three times as much in revenue terms as all the other departments of the Board put together, usually a couple of hundred thousand per year. Then there was the capital, rarely amounting to less than half a million per year. With a budget like that, he had no shortage of visitors wanting to help him spend it. Some hundreds of men were normally employed in the Dock Yard, but at exceptionally busy times the payroll was swelled by short-term 'extra labourers' to over 10,000.

At this point we shall make a small digression. Just up the hill from Brunswick Dock was a rather handsome building, which would soon be both enhanced and expanded, namely the brewery of Daniel Higson, which reminds us of the dozens of pubs and beerhouses along the Dock Road whose importance was touched upon in Chapter 1. To the thousands of sailors to be found in port on any given day, these were places of what might loosely be termed recreation, but to many others — quite apart from the whores and the pimps — they were places of serious business. Tens of thousands of skilled men had regular jobs with ship-repairers, with the Dock Engineer, with gig-boat firms, with carters, with coopers. But trade fluctuated wildly, and there was often a demand for a few extra men on a casual or short-term basis. As usual, lack of security brought enhanced hourly rates. But how, if you needed six journeyman coopers for three days, did you find them? The Ministry of Labour lay far in the future. The answer was that you found which pub the coopers drank in, you went there and you hired them. Carpenters were in another pub, smiths in a third, and so on. There were potentially thousands of journeys on the Overhead involved in this rather anarchic, but highly effective, way of recruiting skilled men for short-term work. Without this 'mechanism' much of the work of the port would have ground to a halt.

Another 701yd on was Toxteth Dock station. This took the railway back into modern docks, for Toxteth and Harrington had been so heavily rebuilt between 1873 and 1888 as effectively to be new

docks. Many and various were the ships and cargoes handled here, but by far the most important were those of (Sir) Alfred Jones' companies, of which Elder Dempster was the most prominent. In the 1890s this was the centre for the West Africa trade, and those who wanted to buy West African produce or to sell to West African markets were on the train for Toxteth. Both Toxteth and Harrington Docks had two-storey transit sheds equipped with travelling hydraulic roof cranes: expensive they may have been, but these were the best cargo-handling kit in the port at the time. Those who wanted their benefits went there.

The original terminus of the railway was almost straight on from Toxteth, a strange elevated predecessor of the Nissen hut standing on stilts and known as Herculaneum Dock station. Herculaneum was originally a general cargo dock, but by the time the railway arrived it had come to specialise almost entirely in petroleum and its products, both in cask and in bulk, and in the loading of cargo and bunker coal. None of these involved really large numbers of men, apart from the coal trimmers, but there were also four graving docks with their usual comings and goings. On the river side was the Dock Board Marine Department's Buoy Store and workshops, while further traffic was generated by the large motive power depot of the Cheshire Lines (CLC) on the inland side. Beyond the MPD, but quite a long walk by authorised routes, lay Grafton Street, the nearest point of a residential district mainly inhabited by the so-called 'aristocracy of labour'. In those days of sectarian division, the people in that area were mostly Protestant, many of them engaged in relatively steady well-paid trades such as shipwrighting or ship-carpentry, which made them good customers as they travelled from one graving dock to another. It was probably the proximity of Grafton Street which first caused the company to look to supply a demand beyond that for which the 'tramnibuses' had catered, namely the ride-to-work market.

There were, it is true, housing areas just inland from the Dock Road for much of its length. They were, however, mostly of unexampled squalor and inhabited literally by those who could not afford to live anywhere better. (Which in effect meant anywhere else at all.) To the unfortunates who lived there, even the 3d for a workman's return on the LOR was too much. They had not been considered as a part of the market for the railway. The message soon dawned, however, that just beyond the ends of the railway there were large quantities of housing occupied by the 'aristocracy of labour' and smaller numbers of houses which might furnish first class passengers. By the time the original line was opened, the Parliamentary powers already existed to build a short extension at each end.

It will be recalled that the line already extended north from Alexandra to the carriage sheds and workshops. Two points, one sharpish turn right, a bowstring bridge over the Dock Road and another 342yd of track sufficed to reach the site which would become Seaforth Sands station, now occupied by the grain silos of Royal Seaforth Dock. The structure was just the same as on the original section, constructed

Above: A northbound train leaving Custom House on the short trip to James Street in the late 1930s. Notice the amazing assortment of 'up-town' warehouses (see Chapter 1) on the right, virtually all of which survived the Blitz. *IAL*

and erected in the same way, though not by exactly the same team: the principal contractor was now Holmes & King of Liverpool. Seaforth Sands station was of unprecedented luxury on the LOR: not only did it have a glazed overall roof, there were even one or two wooden benches provided on each platform. The Northern Extension was passed for traffic and opened on 30 April 1894.

At the south end, the track swung sharply to the left a little short of (old) Herculaneum station, over a lattice-girder bridge crossing the Dock Railway, the 'avenue' inside the boundary wall which divided the Dock Estate from CLC property and some of the CLC ground as well. The bridge was skewed in relation to the obstacles below, so one main beam was 220ft long and the other only 215ft to achieve a clear span of 200ft, easily the largest on the railway. The line then vanished into a tunnel bored into the small cliff which had been created when the site for Herculaneum Dock had been levelled. As Lyster may have told them — he had done the levelling back in the 1860s — it was very nasty red sandstone indeed, and the tunnel had to be brick-arched and lined throughout. There were also difficulties with wet clay beds, which did little for comfort in working during construction and less for stability in the product.

Although the tunnel was only 605yd long (excluding the length of the station at the far end) it proved uncommonly difficult to dig. In addition to the problems already mentioned, there was the Cheshire Lines tunnel underneath, but not nearly far enough underneath. There was, in fact, only 2ft 9in between the crown of the CLC tunnel's arch and the trackbed of the LOR, which meant that the LOR team had to dig down until they found the arch, and then build an arch of their own to carry their trackbed clear (with an air gap) over the lower one. The CLC, in the usual helpful manner of pre-existing lines, pointed out that they had powers to bore another tunnel alongside the existing one to quadruple their track, so the LOR's arch had to have a span wide enough to permit that. What actually happened was that the LOR built a minimal stretch of the new tunnel for which CLC held powers and sprang their arch off it. Almost 40 years after the closure of the Overhead, the former CLC line shows little sign of imminent quadruplification.

Dingle station had its booking hall on Park Road, almost opposite the Ancient Chapel of Toxteth. The area immediately to the north was known as The Holy Land, not through any special piety on the part of its denizens, but because successive streets were named after David, Jacob, Isaac and Moses. It was premium territory for the railway: many hundreds of sturdy recently-built terraced houses (plenty of them still in sound condition today) inhabited by skilled

Above: Looking north from Toxteth station, with the
Cheshire Lines' huge Brunswick Goods Depot in the
background — which is why there is an LNER board on
the platform. *IAL*

craftsmen, clerks, draftsmen and the like. They had
private back yards and their ash bins were emptied
from a back alley. The occupants were families of
some respectability where the main breadwinner
earned perhaps £100 or £120 a year. Railway fares
were not a problem.

At Dingle station the tunnel opened out to a width
of 52ft, sufficient for an island platform, and then
narrowed again to provide a couple of sidings
beyond. From the platform an overbridge led to a
sloping ramp which came up to the booking hall at
street level. It is interesting to note in passing that
the wide portion of Dingle station (which was 163yd
long) was at the time the widest tunnel arch in the
country.

The old Herculaneum station was left virtually as it
stood and used as a carriage shed, and a new
Herculaneum station, about 165yd back towards
Toxteth from the old one, was constructed. This
tapped the traffic of the Grafton Street area by
having a long and rather fragile-looking lattice-
girder footbridge which spanned the CLC main line
and MPD (with a few columns between the tracks).
The extension was opened on 21 December 1896.
The distance of 1,087yd which separated Dingle from

the new Herculaneum station was the largest gap
between any two consecutive stations on the railway.

Attention now moved back to the north end of the
line, where two important connections were made.
At Seaforth Sands, a new station was built, almost
alongside the old one but on the opposite side of
Fort Road, and the track then crossed Crosby Road
South extending 1,047yd to join with the Lancashire
& Yorkshire Railway's route into Exchange from
Southport at Seaforth & Litherland Station. This
passed through a number of areas which might
reasonably be expected to produce first class
passengers. The L&YR was another pioneer of low
voltage electric traction, and the possibility arose of
running through trains from Southport onto the
LOR, to which end the former built some special
lightweight trains, capable of running on the LOR,
at the Meols Cop workshops and the latter started to
change over its pick-up system from the original
channel in the middle of the four-foot to the L&YR
arrangement of flat-bottomed rails in the six-foot,
19.25in out from the running rails. A curious feature
of this extension was that the two stations at
Seaforth Sands, connected by a footbridge across
Fort Road, both continued in use until 1925, when
the last changes to the LOR route were made
necessary by the final stages of the works on the
Gladstone Dock system — including the closure and
demolition of the old station.

Although many further proposals for extensions to,
or connections with, the LOR remained to be made,
only one comparatively modest one was achieved,

Left: View of the new works under construction. The tramway maintenance vehicle is seen parked at the front near one of the trams. *E. Wood & Co*

Below left: Looking north from Herculaneum (new) station. *IAL*

Above right: The view south from Herculaneum (new) station. In the background, the route swings left to Dingle: straight on is the old Herculaneum station, now used as a carriage shed. *IAL*

Right: The CLC motive power depot, showing the footbridge to Herculaneum (new) station. *IAL*

Below: A view from the 'cliff-top' at Herculaneum, showing the bridge and Herculaneum (old) station. *IAL*

namely a short extension which formed a double junction with the L&YR at Rimrose Road. Curiously, this line seems to have been almost exclusively geared to the conveyance of the extraordinary numbers of people heading for the Grand National via Aintree (L&YR Station). When the connection opened in 1906 it was probably of limited use for other purposes, but after the Great War housing began to spring up along much of its route through Aintree to Ormskirk and on towards Preston. It could easily have been a prime commuter route for the LOR — but such an arrangement had little to commend it to the L&YR, whose only competitor in the area was the CLC's Southport-Aintree line. Since CLC's only access to the city centre was by a huge circuit to the east of the city, entering from the south, it made no bad deal for the L&YR to make friends with the LOR: without losing much trade themselves they were able to deny CLC access from the north to the city centre — a denial which would result in the early closure of the CLC Southport line. What is difficult to understand in these circumstances is the failure of the LOR to recognise the strength of its position with three stations serving the commercial heart of the city. It chose to jump into bed with the first suitor, and in the event the L&YR proved worse than unfaithful as its quick and efficient electric service into Exchange hoovered

up traffic from the residential areas at the north end which the LOR might reasonably have expected to gather. A through service from Southport (CLC) to central Liverpool would probably have done L&YR no good at all.

The saddest failure was that of the so-called 'Belt Route' connecting the LOR with the CLC at the south end, enabling it to run right round the east of the city and back to Seaforth. Had this happened, it would have encouraged the connection of other routes resulting in an urban system second only to the London Underground. The expenditure involved would have been trifling compared with that on the government work-making schemes which constructed the East Lancashire Road in the 1920s. The result would not have been just a better transport system on Merseyside, but a network of which the LOR was an integral part. The LOR would probably still be with us.

This short extension to Rimrose Road completed the construction of the LOR and its associated fragments of track. As a result, there was no question of its being any part of the grouping of 1923, for, like the Mersey Railway, it was seen as a line of no more than very local interest. This meant that it would continue to operate as a very small company, possessed of a very small capital, which led to early problems and premature extinction.

Left: Track-level view of Herculaneum bridge and tunnel portal. This is one of the few photographs in which patching of the decking is clearly visible (right foreground). *IAL*

Above right: Seaforth Sands old station in 1924. The lessons of the Dingle fire have definitely not been learned: apart from the timber platforms, barriers, walls and roofing there is even a stack of unused shoring timbers waiting to fulfil the role of the stack of sleepers at Dingle. *IAL*

Right: View from Seaforth Sands new station towards Gladstone Dock. *IAL*

Below: An old postcard view showing the arrangement while both Seaforth stations were working: the new (through) one to the left and the old (terminus) is just visible beyond the tram shed, to the right. *IAL*

Above: A modernised train approaching Seaforth Sands from Seaforth & Litherland. This shows clearly how 'bodging pieces' were used to form curves on straight main girders. *IAL*

Below: A famous fake shot, showing an LOR train on the CLC Gateacre line as part of the proposed 'Belt Route'. The photographer forgot to draw in a conductor rail! *IAL*

The Trains

There were many ways in which the LOR was innovative. One of them was that it may fairly be claimed that it set some basic parameters for the design of light duty urban electric railway systems in this country which endure to this day. In the first place, it removed the motive power from a separate locomotive as used on the City & South London Railway, and placed it underneath the passenger vehicles. Second, it employed a dc supply at comparatively low voltage collected by a shoe running on a conductor rail on the trackbed. Third, at a time when the majority of urban and suburban steam-hauled railways used short carriages carried on four or six wheels, the LOR used relatively long bogie carriages such as were normally associated with prestige mainline trains. Finally, it made its trains fully reversible by having a driving position at each end. These were very simple matters, but they provided the Overhead with a number of important advantages and they formed a model which many others would follow.

Below: A train of original 1893 stock standing at Seaforth & Litherland station. *IAL*

Structurally, the carriages were nothing new: on top of the bogies, or trucks as we should more properly style them, rode a flat bed consisting of longitudinal girders with trussing underneath. On top of this was built an entirely conventional carriage body with ash ribs, tongue and groove planked side skins of teak and a steam-bent panelled roof. Such structures were, if anything, regressive in that their long flat surfaces made them less strong, weight for weight, than the subtly-curved bodies of stage coaches of 80 or so years before. They did, however, provide sufficient strength to carry a lot of people, for people do not weigh much per square foot. They also enabled the use of motorised trucks to provide the clever part of the work.

The motorised truck has a number of possible antecedents, but the Sprague truck, first used on a street tramway in Richmond, Virginia in 1888, may reasonably be claimed to be the parent of the LOR system. It combined drive and suspension systems into a unit which could be placed under almost any vehicle and which could readily be produced in whatever shape and size were needed for any particular application. Mechanically, it was a pretty crude device in that the linear movement from its

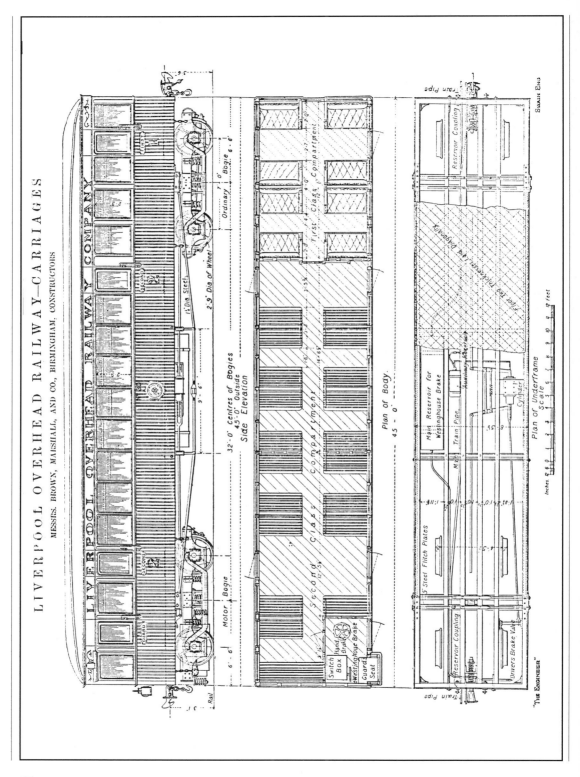

LIVERPOOL OVERHEAD RAILWAY—CARRIAGES

MESSRS. BROWN, MARSHALL, AND CO., BIRMINGHAM, CONSTRUCTORS

suspension deflection had to 'split the difference' around the meshing point of a pair of spur gears. Rewards in this life are rarely given for purity, or the present author would be living in retirement in Mustique instead of scratching crusts by tapping this out on an obsolete word processor: the Sprague truck worked very well. Its real importance did not lie in mechanical detail but in its proof that it was feasible to mount electric motors and their transmission systems on trucks which thus became self-contained propulsion units.

That was the development which clinched the choice of electric power for the Overhead, for it meant that the weight of the motive power could be spread relatively uniformly along the length of the train instead of being concentrated in one part of it in the shape of a locomotive. That was what enabled decisive savings to be made in the cost of the structure of the railway.

The LOR motor coaches not only benefited from the Sprague conception of the self-contained truck but also abandoned its principal crudity: by adopting a form of motor winding devised by Thomas Parker on the basis of earlier work by Thomas Eickemeyer, it proved possible to achieve unprecedented amounts of low-speed torque. This allowed Parker to build the motor armatures directly onto the truck axles. This arrangement was tiresome and costly in maintenance time and tended to unbalance the truck, with too little weight on the non-driven wheels. On the other hand it offered critical advantages: it was simple, quiet and geometrically superior to the available alternatives. Geometry may seem academic, but in the end, bad geometry normally resulted in high maintenance cost as irreconcilable motions were reconciled by the removal of pulverised metal!

Strictly speaking, the LOR control system was not a truly multiple unit system. It was, however, so near to it that we need not quibble. The handle on the controller in the driver's cab was removable, and to drive the train from the other end it was necessary to remove the handle and fit it onto the controller at the other end. This done, the back of the train became the front, eliminating the need both for shunting and for the use of turntables. If only the tramnibus operators had understood the system, they could have effected an amazing improvement in their competitive position by furtively putting a few extra handles into circulation...

The initial stock consisted of 30 motor cars, 45ft long and 8ft 6in wide, made up into 15 two-car trains, of which a maximum of 12 might be in use at any one time. Each train had two 60hp motors (continuous rating 40hp), one on the leading axle of each car. Each train's total power output was thus pretty small beer by steam engine standards. What made the LOR method competitive — or better — was its lighter weight, better weight distribution and

Left & below: Plan, side elevation and section/elevation of one of the first batch of cars. A number of features visible here were soon changed: the couplings were modified, second class became third and the word 'Company' was dropped from the fascia lettering.

The bottom of the diagram left shows the plan of the underframe, original stock, showing the arrangement of the Westinghouse brakes. Notice also the double-diagonal floor planking, presumably intended to enhance torsional stiffness.

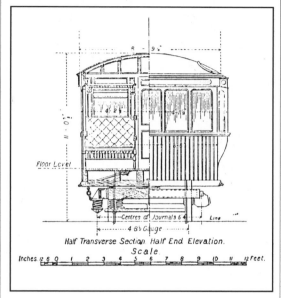

Half Transverse Section. Half End Elevation.

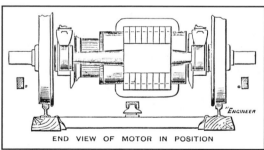

END VIEW OF MOTOR IN POSITION

Above & below: Elevation of 1893-style motor bogie and sketch arrangement of armature/axle assembly.

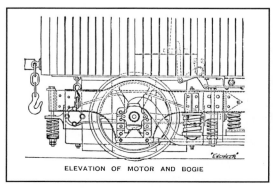

ELEVATION OF MOTOR AND BOGIE

Left: A controller with its cover removed.
IAL

Below: Sketch arrangement of driver's cab from late 1893 (No 31) onwards. *IAL*

Bottom: Pictorial elevation of original stock.

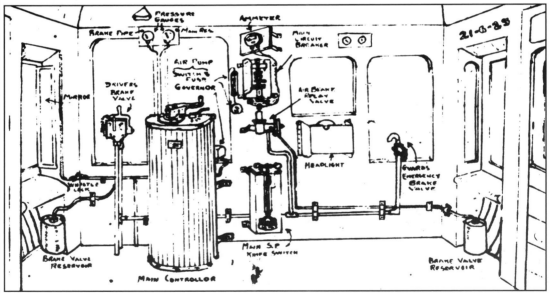

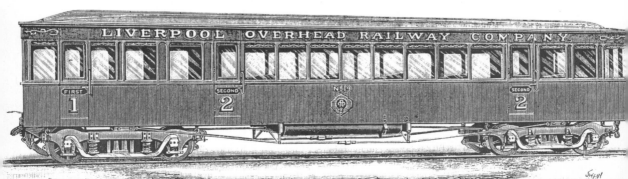

its superior ability to negotiate curves. The original motors, with their amazing low-speed torque, actually proved to be a better bet in many respects than the more sophisticated geared-drive motors fitted at a later stage. They were a little low on power, but one suspects that their main failing was really the fact that armature repairs needed first the dropping of the truck from under the carriage and then the dropping of the axle/armature from under the truck.

The construction of the stock was contracted to Parker's Electric Construction Company of Wolverhampton, but they then sub-contracted the carriage building work to Brown Marshall & Co of Saltley, predecessors of Metropolitan Cammell. The complete bodies were trundled through the streets of Wolverhampton in order to unite them with their bogies. The means by which they were forwarded to the LOR workshops, where the last of their electrical equipment was fitted, has passed unrecorded, but one suspects, given their integral motors and their highly non-standard buffers, that they were carried rather than towed there. On a bolster wagon they might just about have fitted within the LNWR loading gauge. If they did not, heavy road haulage firms like Edward Box would have had no problem in applying their traction engines to the movement of what was, to them, only a 20-ton wooden packing crate. They took plenty of those to Liverpool Docks.

The control system is believed to have been the first to use the 'series/parallel' system. On engaging the first notch on the controller the two motors of the train were connected together in series with two resistances to provide maximum low-speed torque for starting. The next two notches on the controller cut out first one and then both of the resistances. Next, the motors were put in parallel with each other, and finally the resistances were put in parallel with the motors to provide maximum power for what was laughingly known as high-speed running — all of 30mph. The maximum current in what became known as 'full parallel' was about 120A, and suspended from the cab roof was a large electro-magnetic circuit breaker set to 'blow out' at about 160A. In the event of one motor failing and blowing out the circuit breaker, it was possible to disconnect it by means of a simple plug and socket arrangement, to allow the train to crawl on one motor to a rendezvous with the mechanics.

When the control handle was moved, the switch contacts had a sliding motion in relation to each other, which at currents which could exceed 100A was obviously likely to cause arcing. There was no complete answer to this problem, which continued to trouble tram and crane maintenance men for decades, but it was reduced by the provision of a window in the controller which allowed the driver to know what was going on. The changeover from

forward to reverse was effected by a smaller lever on the controller which had a mechanical interlock to prevent it being operated when the main controller was in a position to pass current. Obviously the motors had exactly the same control system and characteristics in reverse as in forward.

The provision of only three spare trains was really a bit mean from the start, for these were rather experimental machines and suffered from lots of minor niggles, including irritatingly short brush life. The extra demands of the Northern and Southern extensions naturally made the ordering of extra stock essential. Late in 1893, eight new carriages, broadly similar to the original stock, were ordered from Parker's Electric Construction Corporation (he had several companies with confusingly similar names). They did, however, exhibit a few minor changes born of experience. The original stock had small rectangular buffers, curved in plan view, mounted on the centre-line. These were generally found to be a good idea, but could override each other and lock on tight curves. The new stock used rather larger buffers of flatter plan which proved much more successful and were later fitted to all the old stock as well. The main difference, however, was a recognition that the 45ft carriages were perhaps a little ambitious in relation to the curvatures of the track: the new stock was only 40ft long. It is interesting, and perhaps surprising, that the shortening was effected entirely between the bogie centres, so that the angular motion at the couplings was actually increased. Clearly that did not prove to be a problem, since no more 45ft stock was ordered.

There seems to have been a mild change in the attitude to passenger comfort in the time between the ordering of the first and second batches of stock. The new stock was some 11% shorter than the old and in the new stock the driver had a full-width cab instead of a tiny cabin of just 5ft by 3ft. These cars were easily recognisable by the fact that they had 'observation bulges' on both sides instead of just the left. The number of passenger seats remained the same at 41 third class and 16 first class: the sacrifice of about 65sq ft of floor space was entirely at the expense of the standing passengers at peak hours, who had to get to know each other rather better.

The third batch of stock was ordered in 1895. Business was quite good, with a total of over 7.5 million passengers in the year and a seat occupancy of about 60%. Within that average figure were hidden a lot of hideously overcrowded rush-hour trains and this, be it remembered, was before the opening of the Southern Extension from which the Company justifiably expected to find many new passengers. The next new stock needed not just to provide more trains, but bigger ones as well. Yet again Thomas Parker got the business, this time under his new incarnation as The Electric

Left: This view of a bogie emerging from the workshops shows the later arrangement, with geared motor drive, greatly improving workshop access, but introducing new problems of its own. *IAL*

Centre left: Interior view, new carriage sheds. Notice that none of the visible fascias has, by this time, any expensive gold lettering or scrollwork. *IAL*

Below: This view of the new carriage sheds, probably taken to mark their opening, includes examples of every variant of stock then in service. *IAL*

Right: Original stock in its final form. *IAL*

Construction Company Ltd. Eight new motor coaches of a broadly similar design to Nos 31–8 were ordered, but there was a completely new departure in the shape of eight trailer coaches to enable the making-up of eight three-car trains. The new motor coaches had 70hp (instead of 60hp) motors to handle the extra weight, but obviously half of the 'new' three-car sets actually used old motor coaches with the 60hp motors. In practice the performance of the 70hp motors was disappointing, so that all the motor coaches for the three-car sets were gradually modified to carry two of the ECC motors each, now mounted on the second and third axles of each car.

Although the trailers were mounted on bogies very similar to those of the motor coaches, they were, at 34ft 6in over buffers, decidedly short. A rearrangement of seating put 40 first class seats in the trailer cars, which left 57 second class in each of the motors. In terms of seating capacity this was a significant improvement, but once again it was achieved at the expense of standing room. The philosophy behind this has passed unrecorded, tempting us to draw the conclusion that it was the off-peak traffic which needed wooing onto the railway because the rush-hour traffic just happened anyway.

It was, however, mainly the rush-hour traffic which tempted a formidable competitor onto the scene.

Liverpool Corporation had municipalised the tramways within its city boundaries, and in 1898 it began to electrify them. Local authorities at that time had a definite unfair advantage in competing with private companies by virtue of the low rates of interest at which they could borrow money. Liverpool was able to borrow money at 3% which it then invested in tramways which produced around 8%: it was this very simple arithmetic which underlay the phenomenal growth of passenger numbers on the Corporation trams. In 1898 electric trams carried 785,064 passengers: by 1900 this had grown to over 58 million and in 1901 it virtually doubled again. The same arithmetic worked in a number of other cities.

In the worst traditions of British transport development, these incredibly successful tram services were not geared to making good deficiencies in a notional integrated 'public service' but to stealing any identifiable traffic already existing. The very first electric tramway route was in direct competition with the LOR's route from Dingle to the city centre. As a producer of short-term financial gain it was a winner, but in overall economic terms it was completely spurious. What made matters worse for the LOR was that the tramways were part of the larger plan of developing municipal electricity generation. In 1898 the main civic and commercial demand was for lighting so that power used, as the tramways used it, mainly during daylight, could be treated almost as a loss-leader to even out the load around the clock, giving the tramways a further competitive — or perhaps one should say uncompetitive — edge.

What could the LOR do in this unequal contest? The Company's answer, probably the only answer, was that because of their railway-standard track they could go faster, potentially much faster, than anything which had to mix it with horse-drawn traffic and pedestrians on the roads. The first stage was the fitting of a three-car set with roller bearings on its axles, which enabled a dramatic improvement in initial acceleration. For a given rate of acceleration it was said to reduce the power requirement on starting by up to 80%. But that saving did not run far: ultimately there was no alternative to the provision of more horsepower. Dick, Kerr & Co, the famous Preston tram-builders, undertook to solve that problem. The roller bearings were soon abandoned because their tracks were found to 'pit' very rapidly on account of return traction currents passing through them.

At one level the chosen solution was brutally simple: three-car sets which used to have either two or four motors of either 60 or 70hp each were now to have four 100hp motors. As one would expect, this made them go much faster: the overall average speed (stops included) with the original stock had been 12.5mph,

as compared with the then fastest elevated railway in the world (Southside, Chicago) at 14.6mph. The prototype for the LOR's upgraded trains averaged very nearly 19mph over the whole route, a truly astonishing figure when one recalls that several of the stations were less than a quarter of a mile apart. The top speed was increased only to 32mph, but of course it was the acceleration which counted, and that reached no less than 4.2ft/sec², corresponding to 0-30mph in 40sec. This was sufficient to cut the total journey time from 32min to under 21.

It was a bold gesture, and the new motors were very cleverly designed. They were, for their day, highly efficient, compact and easy to maintain. Furthermore, compared with their predecessors, they offered a much greater degree of protection against damage to the train in the event of failure or serious overheating. Specifically, the Dingle fire (page 73) would not have occurred with motors of this type. Their problems lay elsewhere. Unlike the original issue motors, which were built onto the axles, the new motors were self-contained units with gear drive to the axles. In service, both the power and the torque of the motors proved altogether too much for the gearing to cope with. Engineers' pocket books used to contain standard tabulated data for the power-handling capabilities of gear trains and it would be interesting to know who it was that thought they knew better. Whoever it was, they were wrong: the 100hp units were a mechanical failure. The motors themselves were good, but because they were good enough to shred the transmission gears, the overall ensemble was poor.

That much one can learn from the 'insider accounts' of Neachell, Rostron and Box, and Box does mention that there were axle failures. The situation was actually worse than has been explained, for these occurrences were fairly frequent and serious. On 21 August 1905, a train derailed at Seaforth Sands, and a week later another one suffered an axle failure, also at Seaforth. On 25 September the same year an axle failure at Huskisson emphasised the dangers. In this case, the train was still moving at some speed when the axle failed, and one of the broken ends got under the return current rail in the middle of the four-foot. There was sufficient momentum in the train to rip the rail up, forcing it through the floor of the carriage and on through the roof. This passage of the rail through the carriage was accompanied by a 'blinding flash of electricity'. Fortunately the train was comparatively empty, and while many people missed death or serious injury by a matter of a few inches, only two men were injured.

Their injuries were slight, and they were, after all, only workmen. We may consider what the consequences for the railway would have been had this accident occurred to the train on which a gentleman who wrote to the *Daily Post* under the *nom de plume* of 'Packed', on 23 February 1903, had travelled. He got on at Huskisson and found all the seats taken and a few people standing. At Clarence a large number of 'cattlemen, labourers and coal-heavers' got on, by which time there were approximately 70 people standing, and 'it took two

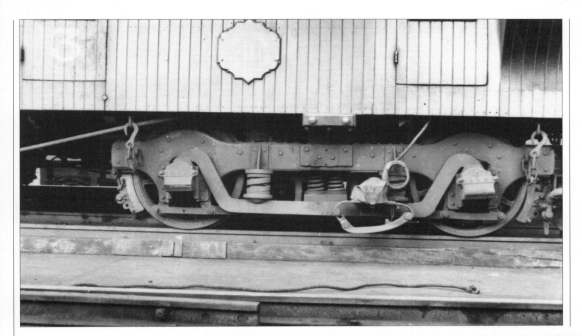

Above left: Ventilation problems led to some stock being fitted with louvred fascias, displacing the company name to a board below the windows. This shot also gives a good impression of just how short the trailer cars were to be riding on eight wheels. *IAL*

Above: The adoption of geared motors made it difficult to move trains around within the sheds. This 500V wandering lead was bolted to the collector shoe to enable limited mobility. *IAL*

Centre right: The interior of a third class car, photographed by C. E. Box in 1935: perhaps best described as practical. *C. E. Box*

Right: A first class interior, photographed on the same occasion. Notice that, despite the comparative elegance, the Company still deemed it necessary to display 'Spitting Prohibited' notices.

men with all their strength two attempts to force the doors to'. There would have been several deaths and dozens of serious injuries.

Sadly, the uprated trains were also a financial failure. They could draw up to 700A per train, a quite ludicrous amount of current when compared with the cut-out setting of the original motors of 160A per train. The remarkable speed of the LOR's up-rated stock undoubtedly wooed back some of the customers lost to the comparatively slow Corpy trams. They did not, however, win nearly enough of them back to pay for the greatly increased coal consumption resulting from the use of the new motors. It was not just that they took a lot of extra power, but that the machine which provided much of that power was the hungry Browett & Lindley unit. The end result was that the percentage of expenses to receipts rose from 58.6% in 1899 to 76.7% in 1905. At the same time, the average 'take' per passenger declined from 2.12d in 1899 to 1.5d in 1906 and the number of passengers continued to decline as well. It seems that the only redeeming merit of the Accelerated Service was that because the trains performed more journeys per day, there was a saving in wages. In 1904, for example, this amounted to £262 on drivers and £379 on guards. It was not as much as the increase in the use of coal and oil, before any of the other problems, such as increased

Above: The third (1895) batch of stock had twin 'look-out pods' protruding from the cab, but they were much more angular than those of the second batch (or, indeed, the single ones of the first batch).

carriage maintenance costs, were taken into account.

One way of reducing the cost penalty of the Accelerated Service was to increase the passenger capacity of the trains, and this was duly tried when 10 of the original 45ft motor coaches were rebuilt with wider bodies. Although the increase was only of 10in, the capacity rose to 60 third class and 19 first. According to Box, it was for aesthetic reasons that these new wide motors were run only as two-car units, and they certainly would have looked a bit odd with a standard-width trailer in between. But if that really was the reason it was an insubstantial one for what amounted to a negation of the purpose of the rebodying exercise, namely that each bunch of four 100hp motors should shift more passengers: two wide-bodied motors did not carry as many as two standard motors with one trailer. Someone, somewhere, was being more economical with the truth than they were with the coal.

The Accelerated Service enabled by the 100hp motors only lasted from 1902–08. In addition to the problems mentioned above, the trains regularly

Above: One of the juggernauts of the LOR, three-car wide-bodied set 27-10-25, seen at Seaforth & Litherland. These cars are easily recognised by the 'tumblehome' which results from their frames remaining standard width. *IAL*

Centre right: 1895 stock 40-3-39 at Herculaneum station, northbound. This is obviously towards the end: there is no lettering at all on the stock, not even to identify the driver's door. *A. F. Porter*

Right: An L&YR 'Dingle Train', southbound at Pier Head station. *J. B. Horne*

suffered hot bearings which are not a mechanical disaster but are pretty bad news for the maintenance of a reliable service. (And that suggests that the experiment with roller bearings had already been written off to experience.) Box attributes the axle failures to track corrugation which, if correct, indicates that the torque reaction of the new motors was causing suspension oscillations. (The springing was by coil springs, which have many advantages but lack the internal damping properties of a leaf spring.) On balance, it is unlikely that this is the correct explanation, since the entire renewal of the track had recently (1903–04) been completed when the cluster of incidents mentioned above occurred.

It seems unkind to say it, but the re-motoring for the Accelerated Service sounds painfully like the once-familiar process of shoehorning a Cortina GT engine into a clapped-out Ford Prefect 100E. It was perfectly possible, and the resulting hybrid went very fast, if only for a short time. The problem was that virtually none of the parts of the Prefect would stand the grunt of the Cortina engine. If the brakes would stand it, the springs and dampers wouldn't, so that it pogoed up and down when you tried your impressive dragster-start in the pub car park. When you put in uprated springs and dampers so the tyres stayed on the ground, the half-shafts sheared. If you wanted to travel at Cortina GT speed, you really had to go and buy a Cortina GT.

Dick, Kerr, it would seem, was not equal to the task of 'tweaking' the work of Parker. The resulting lash-up was unprofitable, unreliable and downright dangerous. As we shall see, it may have had even worse effects on the long-term prospects of the railway. It is unfair, however, to blame the failure entirely on Dick, Kerr, for they were working under instructions from a highly-paid general manager who was considered to be an expert electrical engineer. When an engineer got to be paid more than a thousand or so a year, he was being paid not just for what he did but also for carrying the can. Cottrell was paid £2,200 pa, more than sufficient to justify an expectation that he should be held responsible for an expensive and entirely unsuccessful experiment.

There is just one small problem in such a judgemental approach, which is that even in hindsight it is difficult to imagine what he could have done that might have been more successful — or even less unsuccessful. Staying with what they had was demonstrably not working. Completely new high-speed stock might have been better but was not affordable and would still have placed unacceptable strains on the track and the structure unless it had adopted some entirely innovative form (such as, perhaps, a stressed-skin plywood body) to make a radical reduction in the weight of the stock. Like the joke sticker on the office wall that says, 'The impossible we perform immediately, miracles may involve a slight delay', the Overhead was not short on innovation, but it was put in a situation where only a miracle would allow it to compete with a rival which was allowed to break the supposed rules of the market.

By 1908 failure was acknowledged, and the new controllers which had been fitted along with the GT motors were crudely modified by applying seals which confined them to the series 'notches' — the equivalent of putting a block of wood under the throttle pedal of the Ford Prefect to prevent it being opened more than halfway. The journey time went back up to 28min. There were probably personal factors involved here too, for Cottrell, who had brought the Accelerated Service into being, retired in 1908, the year his oversize motors were restricted, and Edward Neachell, his successor, was an ex-Parker man. But the problems with gears and axles related not so much to speed as to torque and acceleration, so it seems reasonable to assume that three-car trains with the 100hp motors are just as likely to have been eschewed in order to limit torque as for any other reason — except, perhaps, the increased forces acting on the structure. There is no doubt that Neachell was aware of the long-term threat posed by possible overloading of the structure.

In 1917–18 four wide trailer cars were ordered, which enabled the company to put four wide three-car sets into service, and the remaining wide two-car set (Nos 7 and 9) broke the aesthetic rules by forming a set with standard-width trailer No 16. In 1919 business was booming and the decision was taken to re-motor again, though funds did not run to re-motoring the entire stock. The new motors were of 75hp, and to achieve acceleration comparable with the 100hp motors, the gear ratio was reduced from 2.8 to 4.2. The maximum speed fell to a mere 20mph, but the tractive effort on starting was actually slightly higher than from the 100hp motors (13,000 as against 12,000lb) and the rapid initial acceleration which resulted meant that the average speed of the service fell only to 14mph for two-car trains and 13mph for three-car.

The Company did not have anything approaching the resources needed to modernise and standardise everything, so that by the 1920s the stock had become something of a rag-bag assortment. Not only was there a mixture of wide and standard trains, of two-car and three-car sets, but there were also two different classes of motor coach which had not been re-motored: there were two-car trains with two of the 100hp motors and three-car trains with four 100hp motors. The weights of these trains varied between 51 tons 5cwt fully laden for a standard two-car and 75 tons 3cwt for a fully laden wide three-car carrying 291 passengers. It had been the intention since about 1916 to have a standardised stock of

identical three-car units. Some progress was made, and by 1936 all the trains were of three cars, following the conversion of several motors into trailers. Slight slippage occurred in the grander objective of complete standardisation, being still subject to some measure of underperformance at the time of the closure of the railway.

There were three 'oddball' items of stock sometimes to be seen on the railway. The first, and much the best known, was a tiny Kitson 0-4-0 well-tank steam locomotive, built in 1893. No photograph seen by the author shows a nameplate on this locomotive, but she was always popularly known as *Lively Polly*. She was only 15ft 11in long overall and 9ft 4in high, weighing in at just over 10 tons in full working order. Her principal function was to haul a small 'works train' consisting of a four-wheeled wagon and a tool van, though she was sometimes used to haul rails secured on carriage bogies. Her couplings and buffers were LOR-type, and Box records that she sometimes hauled a first class trailer car for inspection purposes when those doing the inspecting wanted to wander about on the track without encountering live rails.

She had an interesting secondary duty, in that she was fitted for carrying a device resembling an overgrown Surform rasp for removing the wrong kind of ice from the conductor rail, and she also had steam pipes so arranged that she could sit on a frozen point and blow live steam on it until it thawed out. On nights when icy conditions were anticipated, a night watchman kept her in light steam overnight ready for work in the very early morning, to allow passenger services to start as usual. It would be interesting to know how many customers the Merseyrail Northern Line has lost through the frequent winter failures at Sandhills Junction because it does not have a Really Useful Engine like *Lively Polly*.

In 1947, *Lively Polly* was deemed to be uneconomic, and was replaced with an equally tiny Ruston diesel 0-4-0 locomotive of only 7 tons 10cwt, which seems never to have acquired a name. (Which brings to mind a bit of doggerel about no diesel being christened Britannia — or Nellie.) After this, there seem to have been occasional problems with icing which involved sloshing various chemicals about. *Polly* was sold to the well-known industrial locomotive dealers Cudworth & Johnson of Wrexham who overhauled her and sold her to REA's for use at their coaling wharf at Monks' Ferry, Birkenhead, where her coal consumption was barely perceptible and the constricted layout of the sidings made a tiny locomotive like her unusually convenient. She lasted as long as the coal traffic there and in 1961 was sold to Central Wagon Company, who broke her up. The Ruston loco was sold along with the rest of the assets when the line

closed. It is an interesting illustration of changing times that it did not feature in the demolition of the structure. Instead of carrying the scrap by rail along the LOR and onto the former L&YR system in a reversal of the construction process, the contractor lifted the pieces down with mobile cranes and removed them by road.

By the end of World War 2, most of the stock of the Overhead was in no fit condition to face a brave new world. The railway had suffered severe damage during the month of May 1941, the Company staff had twice been bombed out of their offices, and the railway had had to fight for its very existence against domestic foes more perfidious and potentially more destructive than the Luftwaffe. Furthermore, when the railway was able to maintain its services, it had abnormally heavy demands placed upon it resulting from the frenzied pace of work along the whole of the Dock Estate. The strain of it all proved too much for Wilfred Box, General Manager and Engineer, who retired in March 1943 and died later that year. It had scarcely been an opportune time for worrying about the generally worn state of the coach bodies, much less about their archaic appearance. Box's successor was a much younger man, H. Maxwell Rostron, who still faced an appalling task in keeping the railway running, but had the advantage of knowing that the worst was over. During 1944 the decision was taken to reconstruct motor No 29 as the prototype for a new postwar image. The original trucks were overhauled and reused, but the body was entirely new (except that in the prototype the old wooden seats were reused).

It is surprising that the Company managed to build this vehicle, for it was aluminium panelled at a time when aluminium was more than a little sought-after for building aeroplanes. (Which, contrary to popular belief, were not in the main made of melted-down park railings.) None the less, it emerged proudly from the workshops and into service in February 1945, complete with a 'bow-wave' paint job of the kind favoured on the Führer's diesel locomotives, on the front panel. While it may have been a largely cosmetic job, it certainly did present a smarter and more modern image than the all-too-obviously wooden original stock with its cluttered rooflines and doors which were close relatives of those used on first class stock on the Liverpool & Manchester Railway in the 1830s. The new styling was still somewhat short of inspired: the modified stock was just as square-fronted and slab-sided as the original and had certainly learned nothing either stylistically or structurally from the sleek-looking LMS units which appeared on the Wirral and Southport lines in 1938. 1946 saw the emergence of rebuilt No 30, which was a more complete and considered job, based on the experience gained with No 29. Gone for firewood were the old wooden seats in the third class, replaced by tubular steel seats with leather upholstery. The complete abolition of roof ventilators in the interests of styling on No 29 was found to have been a mistake and No 30 sprouted some smart new streamlined ventilators. On days when the weather made opening the windows unpleasant, rush hour aboard No 29 must have been an interesting olfactory sensation even to

Above left: Although the Dingle trains were broken up during 1940, this fairly close relative, an ex-L&YR electric baggage car, was spotted in Liverpool Exchange station in 1946. *IAL*

Above: The 'Works Train' delivering materials to a gang between Princes Dock and Pier Head. (Bibby's Oil Mills in the background.) The barrels may well contain bitumen for coating the structure.

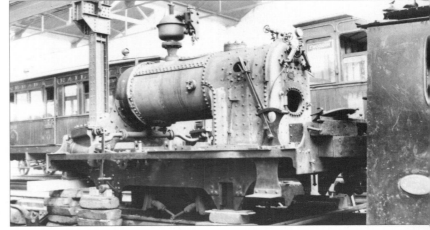

Centre right: Lively Polly undergoing a major overhaul, apparently in the new carriage shed. *IAL*

Right: The end of the line for *Polly*: her LOR-type coupling is on the Ruston, and her buffer beam has been drilled to receive the Ruston's buffers, ready for sale. *IAL*

Liverpudlians, who are mostly fitted with catarrh as original equipment.

In 1947 two complete three-car trains of modernised stock came into service. They were smartly fitted out with plywood interior panelling with matched veneers and stainless steel fittings. The new first class had timber-framed seating with moquette upholstery. The company now began to get ideas above its station and sought quotations for the construction of entirely new trains, intended to consolidate the strengths and eliminate the weaknesses of the seven units so far rebuilt. The price proved totally beyond the means of an impoverished little company, so the decision was taken to continue with in-house modernisation as resources permitted. Considering the limited nature of those resources, the workshops did remarkably well to turn out a complete 'new' train each year until 1955. In general these were the same as the 1947 trains, but a few variations like 'wood-effect' plastic panels crept in.

For such a small company, it was a noble effort. It completed, however, the modernisation of less than half the stock, and a misbegotten assortment of antiquated-looking trains remained. 3-17-13, for example, was virtually original issue apart from its 75hp motors and new(ish) controllers, and the seating capacities varied from 124 in the case of 15-12-16 to 242 in the bulky all-wide-stock trains 6-48-10 and 4-47-17. The wasp-waisted 7-16-19, with wide motors and a narrow trailer, remained in misshapen service to the very end, and to hell with aesthetics.

At the time, the Mersey Railway was carrying phenomenal numbers of passengers in stock, much of it 1903-issue Westinghouse, which looked as though it came from a silent film. The LOR's attempt at modernisation, which even as a partial and cut-

price effort was a considerable strain on the Company's slender resources, did not result in a sufficient growth of traffic to place it on a sound footing to meet the other and larger problems which were looming. On the contrary, traffic stagnated and even declined in some years, leaving the Company with gross annual receipts typically around £150,000. The population of Liverpool was still rising, and so was activity in the Port, but these failed to revive the Overhead. Quite why this should be so, when in the past its traffic had responded fairly quickly and sensitively to the ups and downs of trade, is difficult even for us to understand with the benefit of hindsight. Rostron, his board and his subordinates stood no chance of understanding what was happening and why.

At various stages in the LOR's history there had been ideas of some measure of through running of trains to and from other local lines, and one of these resulted in the construction of a distinctive form of stock. The connection with the L&YR at Seaforth & Litherland offered the opportunity to run trains through from Southport and Aintree along the full length of the LOR to Dingle, and in 1905 the L&YR placed its 'Dingle cars', built at Meols Cop on trucks by Dick, Kerr, in service. There were 12 of these, normally run as six two-car sets, and they used aluminium panelling at that early date in order to get the weight down suffic-iently to allow them to run on the LOR. (Though at 22 tons they were still a little heavier than the LOR's own cars.) The traffic was fairly seasonal, but the cars used a 125hp motor on each bogie, which made them quite powerful enough for use on other routes at times when they were not all needed for use on the LOR, and they ran a good deal between Southport and Crossens. The through services to Dingle were not a great success and were

Above left: The first complete modernised train, 14-7-30, looking extremely shiny in the carriage sheds, presumably just completed in 1947. (The apparent mock-Georgian window is a reflection of the workshop windows, of which the professional photographer should have been profoundly ashamed.) *IAL*

Above: The second modernised train, 15-12-16, at Seaforth & Litherland station. The paint job is slightly different, and all the later cars seem to have had the lighter 'lining', which is in fact an aluminium beading. *IAL*

Right: The modernised third class interior: improved almost beyond recognition, with comfortable seats, grab handles, hanging straps and more standing room for rush-hour passengers. *IAL*

discontinued in 1913, though the L&YR stock continued to appear on the LOR for the Aintree trains for the Grand National and Jump Sunday and also continued a through service as far as Alexandra Dock until after the war. They were broken up in 1940, at the Meols Cop works of the L&YR, probably in order to melt down their wheels to build Spitfires.

Although the LOR generally had an acceptable safety record in relation to train operation, and no cars were 'written off' in collisions (though some needed fairly heavy repairs), a total of nine cars were destroyed by fire in incidents over half a century apart. By far the worst accident to befall the LOR

was the fire which occurred in Dingle station on 23 December 1901, when four staff and two passengers died as the result of a motor failure setting fire to the train 32-5-35. The intense heat set up a flue effect in the ventilating shaft at the end of the platform, with the result that the fire spread rapidly. The train which caused the fire was destroyed, as was a spare train (a two-car unit, 20-22) standing 155yd away in No 4 siding. The accident had a number of causes, including electrical overloading and driver error, but the motor which caused the fire was one of the 'original issue' direct drive ones, which lacked any form of fireproof casing. John Hughes has argued that an unfair share of the

Above: The last days of the LOR: this is the train made up of the 'leftovers' from the Seaforth fire, No 9 of 1893 issue (though shorn of its roof ventilators) and No 10 which was modernised. It is seen southbound at James Street station in October 1956. *A. F. Porter*

blame was attached to the driver, who never spoke up to refute the charges against him: he was dead. One of the key stages in the spread of the fire was the ignition of a large stack of old sleepers which had no business being there. There were, however, at least two further instances of trains attempting to catch fire through electrical overheating and neither appears to have done more than trifling damage: certainly neither was life-threatening, despite the fact that one of them actually occurred in Dingle station.

Perhaps the most remarkable fact relating to loss of stock is that none whatever was lost during the Blitz, despite repeated damage to the structure, to the offices (of which there are some details in Chapter 7) and to property all the way along the route. Many of the raids occurred at times of the day when the trains were still running, but short of parking them all in the Dingle Tunnel they were still very much in the firing line after services had ceased for the night anyway. In so far as the Luftwaffe had the faintest idea where bombs would actually land, both Seaforth Sands station and Herculaneum Carriage Shed were close to particularly choice targets, namely Gladstone Graving Dock and the Herculaneum and Parkhill oil depots respectively.

The second fire was at Seaforth Sands station in the small hours of 4 February 1956, as the result of arson by persons unknown. Given the state of the company's finances at the time this might encourage a certain amount of eyebrow-raising, but realistically the insurance money from a localised fire such as this would have made no difference to the overall situation. Two three-car trains were, as usual, standing in the station ready to run the first services of the morning, and motors 2 and 12 and trailers 4 and 6 were totally destroyed. This led to the impromptu creation of a two-car train with what was left, namely motors 9 and 10, 10 being modernised and 9 not. But by then the railway had less than a year to run, so who cared? It is also interesting to note that Box records in passing that the insurance value of a three-car train at the time was 'about £10,000' — without differentiating between modernised and unmodernised stock!

Chapter 6
Signalling

The ideas that Alfred Holt had for doing away with signalling costs entirely may have proved unacceptable, but by virtue of its all-electric operation the railway still offered scope for all-electric signalling, which promised to be both economical and innovative. The company adopted I. A. Timmis' electric block system, which allowed signalmen to be dispensed with throughout the route apart from two small boxes at the termini. The signals were of conventional semaphore type, but electrically actuated and controlled by the movement of the trains themselves. This was how it worked. Each station had two signals (for each track): a home and a starter. When a northbound train stood boarding passengers in, say, Pier Head station, its starter was normally showing 'clear' and both the home of Pier Head and the starter of James Street would be showing 'danger'. When the train started, it set the Pier Head starter to 'danger' and, about two train lengths later, it tripped a contact to set both the Pier Head home and the James Street starter to 'clear'. The circuit which needed to be completed to change those signals to 'clear' also passed through a mercury switch on the arm of the Pier Head starter. If it, for any reason, had failed to move to 'danger', the circuit remained uncompleted, so that the signals in rear remained at 'danger'. Any failure of wiring or power supply would cause the signals affected to fail safe and indicate 'danger'.

The supply and installation was contracted, once again, to the ubiquitous Thomas Parker, this time in his guise as the Electric Construction Co, but he sub-contracted the work to the Railway Signal Company at Fazakerley. In the arrangement they adopted, the signal arms were pulled to the 'clear' position by long-pull electro-magnets which were fitted with an ingenious current-saving device: although it took 5A to move the arm, once it had moved, it made a contact to switch in a resistance so that only 0.25A would suffice to retain it at 'clear'. All the making and breaking contacts were duplicated, as were the lamps of the signals, and the power supply came from duplicate 50V accumulators, of which one was in service while the other was free to be charged as necessary. The original charging arrangement involved charging batteries in series from the traction supply, which must have involved some fairly cunning communication routine in order to have the right number of batteries in circuit at any one time. In early days, the voltage of the traction supply varied a little as well: during normal running it was typically around 485, but could reach 530, a variation large enough to make a material difference to the charging rate of the batteries. Not suprisingly, this cheap but rather erratic method did not last long before rotary converters driven from the traction supply were applied to charging duties. The batteries

Below: One of the original electro-magnetic signals working on the Timmis principle.

also provided the power for station lighting except at Dingle, where it worked direct from the traction supply.

The signals looked safe on paper, and were, obviously, approved by the Board of Trade before the opening of the railway, but in practice there were some teething troubles. In the second half of 1893, signals refused to go to 'clear' on 1 in every 1,200 operations, which sounds quite good until we realise that over 200 trains passed through every station every day and each time a train went through a station there were three 'signal operations'. In other words, signal failures occurred very roughly at the rate of 0.5 per station per day. That was a source of delay and irritation, but in one case in 24,000 a signal failed to move to 'danger'. Given the density of the traffic and the number of signals along such a short line, this means that a highly dangerous situation arose approximately every other day at some point or other on the route. Expressed like that, it sounds less comfortable than it does according to the 1 in 24,000 approach, but then that was published by S. B. Cottrell, and he would put it that way, wouldn't he? Come back, Alfred Holt…

The distressing possibilities of such failures were not ignored, and a number of minor improvements were made over the years. In 1897 each station was equipped with a Sykes semaphore bell block instrument and the station staff were required to keep a train book recording the times at which the trains were indicated by the instruments. At the busiest times, with up to two instrument indications per minute to enter in the book, the staff can have had little time to spare for customer care. This was an important conceptual change, for the time being, as it ended the idea that the trains could entirely control themselves. In effect the railway now had a signalman at every station, even if, one suspects, he was not getting paid the rate for the job.

The next significant change was the abolition of the low-voltage battery operation. As might be expected, after a few years there were occasions when flat batteries caused signals to fail safe and stop the trains. Cottrell remained faithful to the Timmis principle as modified with Sykes instruments, but in 1902–03 he changed the whole system over to operation at traction voltage. The old 'break' contacts which set signals to 'danger' were now placed in the four-foot. The 'make' contacts, which set signals to 'clear' made use of the fact that, to be able to run wrong road, the trains had twin collector shoes. The 'spare' collector shoe energised the 'make' contact as the train passed. The common return wire which had been used with the old system was dispensed with; at the much higher voltage now employed, the running rails were perfectly capable of serving as the return. The result was a system which was not only more reliable, but simpler as well: faults became less likely

to occur and also easier to diagnose if they did.

Or so it appeared. In fact it introduced one critical weakness which seems not to have caused any trouble for 15 years — though in the light of hindsight it is difficult to know why it took so long. The change was a simple enough one, in that instead of the arm being held at 'clear' electrically as described above, a small pawl engaged to hold it there mechanically. That simple change meant that the fail-safe property of the original Timmis system was lost: a mechanical failure resulted in the signal staying at 'clear' rather than defaulting to 'danger'. In 1915, Edward Neachell, Engineer and General Manager, gave a paper to the Liverpool Engineering Society. In the discussion, one member enquired further about the signalling system, stating that:

'He did not remember ever seeing a signal standing at "danger" although he had waited for the next train to his destination to observe if any action of the signal took place.'

Mr Neachell's response was reported thus:

'He did not quite understand Mr Mills' remarks about the signals not going to "danger". They ought always to go to "danger" and in most cases they did so. The percentage of failures was very small indeed.'

One wonders what he meant by a very small percentage indeed. 0.1% is quite a small percentage, but such a failure rate would suffice to leave a train with its rear unprotected on average about four times per week.

By the time Neachell gave his paper, further minor alterations had been effected. In 1914, traffic was good and the possibility of closer headways at peak times became attractive. The problem was the large variation in distances between the stations. The shortest, James Street to Custom House, was only 274yd, while in four cases adjacent stations were over 1,000yd apart. The answer was found in placing 'outer home' signals 200yd in rear of the 'inner home' signals on four of the longer sections. (What was wrong with the word 'distant' is unclear.) This provided an added safeguard in case of signal failure, driver error or poor visibility, and automatic train stops were also added in an attempt to eliminate entirely the risk of collision due to driver error. These first train stops employed a pick-up brush on the front of the train, which would meet a live trackside contact if the signal had been passed at 'danger'. The completion of this circuit both cut off the power to the motors and applied the brakes.

The train stop arrangement also contained a potentially dangerous flaw. When the power was switched on in the morning the signals would (or should) all be at danger, and the means of setting

Above: LOR train circuit breaker of 1892 which was mounted on the inside of the roof in the driver's cab.

Below: Signalbox A, outside Seaforth Sands station. *IAL*

them ready for the running of the first train was to run a pilot train which passed all the signals at 'danger', making and breaking all the appropriate contacts as it went. This had been the procedure from the very beginning, but at the beginning the system had not relied on train stops as part of its safety equipment. How did the pilot train now do its duty, if it could not pass a signal at 'danger' without getting stopped? It was easy enough: all it took was a push-button in the cab which the driver held down to break the stopping circuit and then he could drive over train stops. It does not appear to have occurred to anyone that a driver might use this facility when he believed, in good faith, that a signal had failed and thus put his train at risk of collision.

Of course in real life it was nowhere near as dangerous as it looks on paper because of the short distances and low speeds involved. Most potential collision situations involved a risk of running into the back of a train standing in a station, so the train which had got where it should not be would in any case be braking for the station. Train weights were low, and the Westinghouse compressed-air brakes were effective, so that a signal failure was most unlikely to lead to a collision except in the presence of at least one other hazard — such as a good old-fashioned pea-souper smog. Liverpool was justly nicknamed 'The Windy City', and hence suffered from smog relatively infrequently, but when the wind dropped and it it did get one, it got it just as badly as any other major city, with visibility down to a few yards for days on end. Although the teething troubles with the signals were mostly mechanical rather than electrical, and the incidence of failures was rapidly reduced, there remained a small number

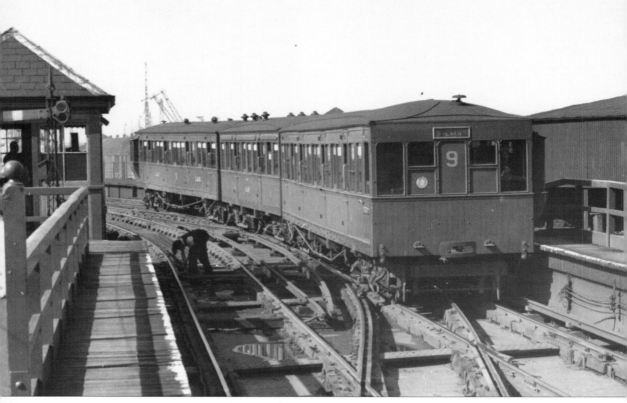

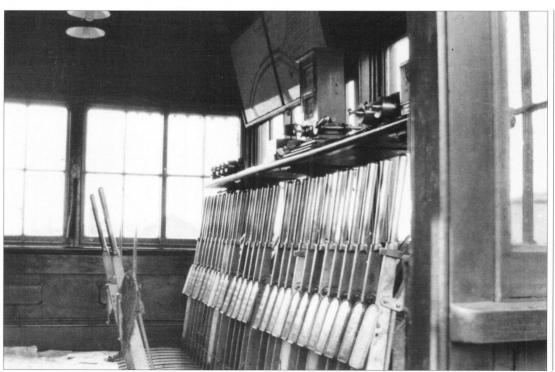

Left: A train bound for Seaforth & Litherland entering Seaforth Sands (new) station, passing Box A. *IAL*

Below left: The interior of Box A: the functions of the levers are shown on the diagrams. *IAL*

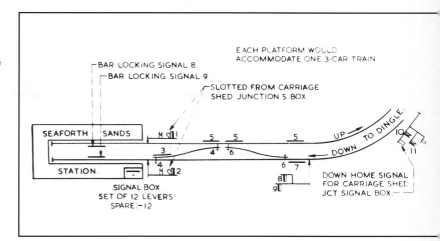

EACH PLATFORM WOULD
ACCOMMODATE ONE 3-CAR TRAIN

BAR LOCKING SIGNAL 8.
BAR LOCKING SIGNAL 9
SLOTTED FROM CARRIAGE
SHED JUNCTION S BOX

SEAFORTH   SANDS

STATION.

SIGNAL BOX
SET OF 12 LEVERS
SPARE :- 12

UP   TO DINGLE
DOWN

DOWN HOME SIGNAL
FOR CARRIAGE SHED
JCT SIGNAL BOX —

Above right: The signalling arrangement for Seaforth Sands (old) station. The old carriage shed is further towards Dingle, and is not shown. *IAL*

Centre right: Signalling arrangement after the opening of the new station at Seaforth Sands, the old station being retained for trains terminating there and as a carriage shed.

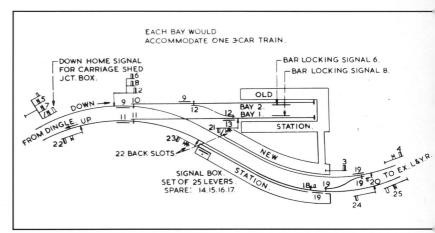

EACH BAY WOULD
ACCOMMODATE ONE 3-CAR TRAIN.

DOWN HOME SIGNAL
FOR CARRIAGE SHED
JCT. BOX.

BAR LOCKING SIGNAL 6.
BAR LOCKING SIGNAL 8.

OLD

BAY 2. BAY 1.

STATION.

FROM DINGLE   UP
DOWN

22 BACK SLOTS

SIGNAL BOX.
SET OF 25 LEVERS.
SPARE: 14.15.16.17.

NEW

STATION

TO EX. L.&.Y.R.

Below: The semaphore signals at Seaforth, shown here in a 1920s view, remained until the closure of the line. *C. E. Box*

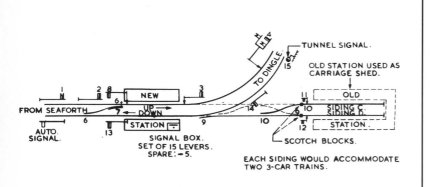

of occasions of which it could be said that the signalling system had not made an accident impossible. When trains could run as often as every 2½min at busy times, that was probably unacceptable. The railway successfully rode its luck until 1919, when two almost identical accidents occurred. Both involved a northbound train running into the back of one which should have been 4min ahead and wasn't, both happened in fog, and both happened within the space of a month. Neither damage nor injury was severe, but the coincidence of one spell of bad weather producing two potential disasters was enough to consign the Cottrell-Timmis system to the scrapheap. As if to emphasise the point, on 25 January 1921, while the work of installing the new system was still in hand there was another slight collision. This one resulted from a driver being wrongly given a green hand signal, whereupon he used his handy push-button to drive over the train stop.

It must be emphasised that the overall safety record of the LOR was quite good. The job of the railway inspector, however, is not to give thanks for past deliverance but to attempt to foresee and forestall possible future causes of disaster. In 1919 the writing was clear on the wall, and the report on the accidents by Colonel Pringle was not very complimentary:

'The evidence in those two cases shows there is much to take exception to in many directions in regard to automatic signalling on this electric railway. The failures of the mechanical replacers (the devices which released the pawls to set the signals to "danger") appear to be numerous.'

The train-stop system was criticised for having several possible causes of failure, and for having the override button placed where a driver could reach it rather than where it had to be operated by an inspector or other responsible person. Train stops needed to be provided at all fixed signals. It was also possible for a signal which had been passed at 'danger' then to set itself to 'clear'. In fog this could have enabled an horrific three-train pile-up, although, of course, it never actually did. The Sykes two-position block instruments were considered old-fashioned and unsatisfactory and the instructions for their use for the acceptance and dispatch of trains no better. 'Irregularities in working the bell code have developed.' Partly as a check on this, there was a requirement that each station and the two signalboxes should be equipped with telephones.

The Colonel recommended that if reliable mechanical replacers could not be made, then the system must revert to the old all-electric operation of the Timmis system. He clearly did not think much of the Cottrell hybridised system. His report really amounts to a recommendation that a completely new signalling system was needed, except for the bits at the ends of the line, where the mechanical semaphore signals could be allowed to remain. Surprisingly, he did not seem unduly concerned about the fact that there were no standard timepieces, but in 1921 the Company installed a 'master and slave' system to ensure that staff at the stations and the signalboxes were all working to exactly the same time.

The severe criticisms in the report seem fair, for the risks were high: had a train failed on a foggy day in a section where the signals were not protecting it, it could have been run into by a train under power rather than one which was already most of the way to stopping at the time of the impact. Both the 1919 accidents occurred in the morning rush hour, and the consequences of a 'real' collision — crushed timber coaches containing hundreds of people, damaged cables, fire, pieces falling over the sides of the structure — could not be contemplated.

The report on the 1920 accident specifically states that had the new system been complete and in action the accident would have been impossible.

It may seem surprising that a company as innovative as the LOR had not adopted track circuiting from the start, for by the time decisions were being made track circuiting was fairly well established in America and there were a few examples of its application in Britain. It was not, however, a well-known and accepted system at that time, and problems were anticipated because the running rails served for the return side of the traction current. In 1920 the track circuit's time arrived, and agreement was reached with the McKenzie Holland & Westinghouse Power Signal Company for the installation of the new system at a cost of nearly £20,000. Where the Company did regain its reputation for novelty was in the signals themselves, which were the first long-distance daylight colour light signals in this country. Fears that they might not be readily visible on sunny days were soon dispersed, and *The Engineer* published a photograph in which a signal light was clearly visible at 1,000yd, or roughly 10 times the braking distance of a train. They emphasised that the negative had not been retouched. (But it was probably ortho-chromatic film!) Special care was apparently taken in the production of the colour lenses to achieve density and permanence of colouring, which was considered important in case any of the drivers might have a 'tendency towards colour blindness'! Unconscious black humour apart, this was a potentially serious matter: while the colours of

Victorian church windows seem to keep quite well, it is not uncommon to see cars on the road whose brake-light lenses have so faded as to be mistakable for reversing lights.

The bodgery of batteries charged from the traction supply was long forgotten as ac made its appearance: two 25kVA rotary converters driven from the main traction supply in the generating station provided a 600V 50 hertz supply. This relatively high voltage, adopted for covering the distances without undue losses, went into transformers at each station to provide the 100V supply to the signals, the 6V track circuit supply and an 11V supply as well. Each signal lamp had a 12V bulb at the focal point of its reflector, with a completely independent 110V bulb behind it as a back-up. An interesting constructional quirk is that the cables running north and south from the generating station were continuous lengths: mechanically speaking, they passed straight through junction boxes.

When a train passed a signal, it set it to 'danger' and it remained thus until the train had passed the next signal by an overlap distance of 100yd, corresponding to the braking distance of a train which had passed a signal at 'danger' and hit the train stop. The system actually allowed trains to run safely with only one signal protecting their rears, for a train could leave a station when there was still a train in the next, with just the 'home' of the next station set at 'danger'. This meant that the extra protection of the train stop and its overlap was extremely important, and a new form of train stop was used. It was operated by an ordinary signal

motor, and when its signal was set to 'danger' it turned its arm towards the rails. A train attempting to pass at 'danger' struck the stop with its trip valve, which simultaneously blew out the main circuit breaker and applied the brakes. If this seems rather minimal protection, it should once again be remembered that we are talking about a railway where the average speed was about 14mph and where unless it was foggy it was mostly possible to see if there was a train in the next station from the position of the previous signal.

As an entirely additional protection, each signalbox now had an illuminated track diagram indicating which sections had trains on them and which did not so that station staff in any doubt about dispatching a train could double-check by telephone.

Box describes the mathematical processes by which the positions of the new signals were determined, a level of detail which need not trouble us here, but it is worthy of mention that they not only allowed further shortening of the headway to 2min, but also allowed a factor of safety even at that frequency by virtue of having been calculated on the basis of a 100sec headway. The retention of the manual boxes at the ends of the route made this less complicated than one might expect, as the new system only applied to the 'straight' track between Alexandra and Herculaneum, but even on the easy part there were crossovers at six of the stations, which worked on a semi-automatic system. A lever on the platform both operated the points and fed the necessary electrical indication to the signalling system for it to set the appropriate signals to 'danger'. They in turn fed back a current to illuminate a lamp by the lever which showed that the signals had done what they should

Above: One of the station crossover levers. *IAL*

Below: One of the new colour light signals with the covers of its control gear removed. *IAL*

have. In 1925 the new system was extended to Seaforth Sands and finally in 1945 to Dingle, making the entire line fully automatic apart from the relatively infrequent crossover, shunting and shedding movements. While on the one hand this may be seen as an improvement, it was probably also a worthwhile economy, for it saved four wage packets. It may be mentioned in passing that although the boxes were only small, they were pretty busy places: Box calculated that in a normal 16hr day (two 8hr shifts) under the old system there were 2,728 lever movements to be made in the Seaforth box. The only other significant change was that enforced by the closure of the generating station, when the little building known as 'signal house' was erected at Bramley-Moore to house the rotary converters, which now drew their supply from the track feeder cables.

The reader who has been paying proper attention and remembering all the extra bits of wire being added on for signals, clocks, telegraphs, telephones and the like may by now be wondering how the problem of the movable bridges was overcome. The answer was with some difficulty: it took about 45min to make the necessary disconnections and the same to reconnect afterwards. This is, of course, the reason why the bridges were opened as little as possible, and not at all during the daytime. That is in turn one of the reasons for the extraordinary attempts to close down the Overhead during World War 2, recently discovered by Maund. The Dock Board, on the other hand, was able to turn this obstruction to advantage: for many years Stanley, the most awkward dock to get in and out of, was a favourite place for berthing vessels which were under arrest or distraint. There are still ex-dockers around who call it 'the prison dock'. In the latter days of the Overhead the opening of the bascule bridges was such a tedious business that shippers sometimes found it cheaper and easier to hire the Dock Board's 200-ton floating crane Mammoth. For loads under 60 tons she could use her 'little' auxiliary block with a reach of 60yd and lift things clear over the line.

During my childhood, the Overhead was legendary for its ability to carry on running in appalling weather conditions, and especially in the smogs which still occurred. The ferries had their radar system (installed in 1947, this was the first such civilian installation) and also ship-to-shore contact with the Port Radar Station so that they could operate almost completely 'blind', but everything else virtually stopped, sometimes for days at a time. Box was able to recall a memorable smog in 1929 when absolutely everything except the Overhead stopped. The LOR's combination of relatively visible signals, lack of junctions, slow speeds and effective train stops allowed drivers to continue working in conditions which were almost impossible for any other form of transport. That it should continue to do so on the strength of a system over 30 years old and whose basic principles were 70 years old says much for the new installation of 1921. It does not say so much for other railways in the area, some of whose signalling systems would have been readily comprehensible to a Victorian country blacksmith.

Below: A modernised train leaving James Street, with the 'home' for Canning (formerly Custom House) already clearly in view. *J. F. Davies*

84

Chapter 7

The Route to an Early Grave

At the time of writing, Radio 4 broadcasts a comedy series entitled 'If you're so clever, why aren't you rich?'. This is actually quite a fair question to ask of the Overhead Railway, with its string of technological firsts. Coupled with the enormous potential traffic which brought it to birth, it should have made a lot of money, or so it might appear. In fact, shares in the Overhead proved to be a very poor investment.

The Company was never rich: the initial intention of Alfred Holt had been to build something radically cheaper than conventional railways, and while the eventual product cost more than he had intended, it was always an undercapitalised line built on the cheap. The adoption of electric traction was to save money on the structure, the electric signalling was adopted because it promised to be cheaper than a traditional mechanical system and the Hobson decking was a really clever piece of cost-cutting. The result was that a technically very demanding line was completed and opened on the strength of a share capital which eventually grew to £658,620 and a debenture issue of £168,880. The total cost of the original length of the structure was £466,000, about £80,000 per mile, which was only about 2.5 times the average cost of an ordinary railway built on the ground. The problem arose in the fact that the ground on which ordinary railways are built is not normally subject to constant deterioration and therefore in need of constant maintenance. That would not be an insuperable problem if it were budgeted in from the start, but it rather seems that the Company failed to realise this. Certainly its revenues were never adequate for the purpose, despite its success in carrying more passengers than were originally deemed necessary to render the operation solvent.

There had been various numbers of passengers bandied around as being the minimum needed to make the railway viable, of which Lyster's 1885 figure of 8,000,000 was about the most pessimistic.

Left: The last of the genre. Again almost all the ships are passenger liners and the arrangement of the dock entrances beggars description. The train may have some difficulty getting to Gladstone Dock station without any conductor rail ahead of it. *IAL*

This total was achieved by 1897 and in 1914 the 10,000,000 mark was passed. Even in the lean years of the early 1900s, the numbers remained around 8,000,000. With up to 25% more passengers than supposedly necessary, how could it fail? Unfortunately, it was quite easy. When Neachell read his paper to the Liverpool Engineering Society it was discussed along with a paper by Joshua Shaw, Chief Engineer of the Mersey Railway. One of the comments offered in the discussion was that the Mersey and the Overhead seemed alike in that while passing through areas of very large population, they both lacked length and both started nowhere in particular and ran to nowhere in particular. While Shaw agreed with this in so far as it applied to the Liverpool end of the Mersey Railway, Neachell avoided either answering or commenting. It was a question which the Company needed to address urgently, because not many people wanted to go from Seaforth to Dingle, and the average value to the company of each passenger carried declined from very nearly 2d in 1897 to less than 1.7d by 1913. What's 0.3d between friends? When you have 10 million customers, it's about £12,500. Gross receipts in 1913 were under £80,000, a sum to which that £12,500 would have been a more than useful addition.

The introduction of the electric trams, which were much slower than the LOR but carried passengers for around half the price, caused a sharp decline in passenger numbers between 1899 and 1902 from 9.6 to 8.5 million, and since the fare structure remained the same, the gross receipts took a similarly alarming dip. The following year saw an encouraging rise as a result of the introduction of the Accelerated Service, but while the passenger numbers then meandered around a mean of about 8.8 million, receipts tailed off at the same time that costs were rising for the reasons given in Chapter 5. One factor in these rising costs arose from changes made to the fare structure in an attempt to woo back lost custom.

When the railway opened, it followed the Alfred Holt idea of simplifying everything, and made a flat-rate charge of 3d first class and 2d third class for any distance, with a cheap workman's return available at 3d before 8.00am. It was not even necessary to issue a ticket for third-class singles, since the fact of having passed through the turnstile was proof of

Above: Like the others, this poster of the early 1930s is pretty inaccurate, with particular reference to the plethora of passenger vessels and almost complete absence of the cargo liners which were Liverpool's principal traffic. *IAL*

Overhead, trying to compete, it was actually even worse than that. The LOR had to pay rates on its premises. In the years between 1900 and 1914, these typically amounted to a little over £4,000 pa, roughly equal to half the working profit in one of the worse (but not worst) years. The Corporation tramways did not, of course, have to pay rates on their extensive depots or on their generating capacity. They also took full advantage of the ability which the extent of their system gave them to indulge in predatory pricing. Thus when the LOR gained its connection to Seaforth & Litherland station the tram fare from Litherland to Pier Head was immediately reduced from 3d to 2d. It is unlikely that the trams covered their costs at 2d, but they could be propped up by the surplus profits from some other route on which there was no competition. Liverpool Corporation was very familiar with these techniques: it had been trying since the 1860s to get their employment by mainline railway companies made illegal.

The trams had other advantages, notably the fact that they could offset their slowness by the convenience provided by their very frequent stops and the large numbers of cars in service. Tram stops could easily be moved if a new connection or some change in local demand required it, whereas the moving of an Overhead station was quite a major undertaking. More than once in the Chairman's Reports in the years 1900–14 we find that the ritual apology to shareholders for another bad year was followed not only by complaints about the unfair competition of the trams but also by the statement that had 'present conditions' obtained at the time the railway was first suggested, it would never have been built. In short, years before the peak number of passengers was carried (22,000,000 in 1919), gentle hints were being dropped that the railway was fundamentally unviable.

'Present circumstances' included much more than just tramway competition. The reader will recall that the outline of the need for the railway given in Chapter 1 mentioned the large numbers of messenger boys and clerks needing to travel. The telephone was already in use in Liverpool before the railway was built, but relatively few people were connected, and it seems to have been regarded with some suspicion as a newfangled gadget which might never catch on. There is great irony in the fact that a telephone call to London featured in the opening celebrations of the railway, as a demonstration of the wonders of electricity. By 1910 at the latest, the telephone was doing serious damage to the traffic on the railway as boy messengers were increasingly supplanted by female telephonists who transmitted messages without leaving the offices of their employer. By 1914 this was publicly acknowledged by the Company as a significant cause of their problems.

payment; only first class, return and prepaid passengers needed the Company to incur the expense of providing a ticket. But when the electric trams arrived, they charged 1d for any journey inside the old city boundary — within which lay 10 of the 17 stations of the LOR. A system of fare stages, at 1d per stage was therefore adopted, which still left the LOR more expensive than the trams for many journeys, but relied on the fact that people would pay a little extra for the faster service. (Which, as we have seen, some would and did.) But the new system not only reduced the earnings per passenger, it also increased the costs of issuing, inspecting and collecting tickets. There had been much talk of 'the magnetic penny', meaning the psychological appeal of a penny fare, but the attraction proved insufficient.

As explained in Chapter 5, the Corporation tramways enjoyed unfair advantages in the cost of borrowing money and the cost of electricity. For the

Above: There is no doubt that 'tourism' worked for the railway. Here, Huskisson station is crowded with school parties. *IAL*

Below: Assorted workers waiting to board a northbound train at Gladstone Dock. Unfortunately it took a lot of school parties to make much impact on a lack of people like these, who travelled not once a term but twice a day. *IAL*

GLADSTONE DOCK LIVERPOOL
LARGEST GRAVING DOCK IN THE WORLD
(IN COURSE OF COMPLETION)
VIEW FROM THE OVERHEAD RAILWAY AT SEAFORTH SANDS

These were troubled years of change in the shipping industry as well. There was a tendency both for companies and their ships to become larger in size and fewer in number. This in itself reduced the number of people needing to move up and down the line of docks. More and more of the work was done at the 'appropriated berths' of the major liner companies, which meant that gangs of dock labourers needed to move around less. The largest passenger liners began to coal in the river, and while there were only a few of them, the thousands of tons of coal they shipped for each voyage made them major consumers, and the men who loaded and trimmed the coal were removed from the railway. The hundreds of shore-based cleaners who rendered the ships ready for their next voyage were likewise travelling to and from their work by boat rather than by Overhead.

Another major traffic which declined seriously was the ship-repairers' men. When the railway opened there were some 20 graving docks, mostly designed to hold two or three ships in line astern, along its route. These too were affected by the 'fewer and bigger' phenomenon: when the five Sandon Graving Docks went, only one new one, at Canada Dock, was built. The Queens Graving Dock of 1908 replaced four smaller ones. The reasons are many and complex, but at the risk of oversimplifying, there were fewer wooden ships in service; anti-fouling paints were getting better all the time; ships were generally more seaworthy and thus less likely to arrive in port damaged. The ship-repairing industry

Above: The Gladstone Graving Dock was the biggest in the world for a time, and the LOR provided a commanding view of famous liners and the occasional battleship or aircraft carrier using it. *IAL*

itself became more efficient, and all these changes taken together made serious inroads into the thousands of scalers, painters, stagers, shipwrights, carpenters, boilermakers and fitters needing to use the railway to get from their depots to the graving docks and from one graving dock to another. Because fewer ships were spending less time in the graving docks, fewer crew members had less free time in port to use the railway to visit the fleshpots.

All this presented a grim and worsening picture for the shareholders of the LOR. When the negotiations were proceeding for the Company to take over the Dock Board's powers to build the railway, much thought and argument went into the question of profit. The Board felt it was sailing a bit close to the edges of its statutory powers by investing in the railway (which, technically, it probably was). Eventually it was agreed that profits above those corresponding to a dividend of 6% on the ordinary stock should be regarded as 'excess profits', and special arrangements were made for their division. Between 1900 and 1914 the dividend never exceeded 1.5%, and in several years no dividend at all was paid. The value of the £10 shares fluctuated between about £3 and about £1 2s 6d, representing a serious

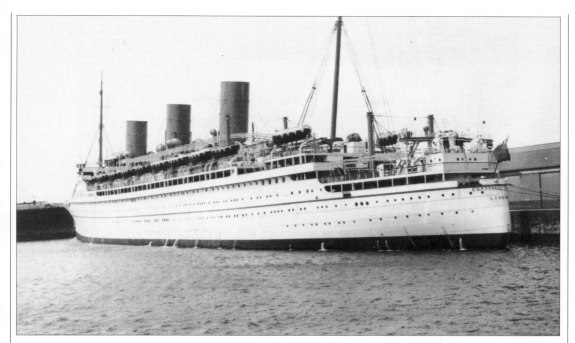

Above: Of course, there genuinely were large passenger liners using the docks as well, and many of them were very pretty vessels. *IAL*

Below: This is what the view was really about, though. A couple of very ordinary ships, and lots of goods moving about. The photographer has cheated a bit by utilising the extra height of the footbridge at Gladstone station. *IAL*

loss to those unfortunate enough to have bought at par, as many had. The directors never lacked advice from shareholders who wanted either to cut fares to gain volume at the expense of profit or to raise fares to gain profit at the expense of volume. They vacillated a certain amount, but in effect both policies were tried and both failed.

1914 was a good year, but that was no consolation to shareholders, for 1914 was a good year for shipping and the general trade of the Port. It had been painfully apparent from about 1905 onwards that the fortunes of the railway depended intimately and directly on the general state of trade in the Port. Nothing the Company could do actually made any real difference. If shipping and trade were bad, then fare cuts might slow the diminution of traffic at the expense of profitability, but the fact was that in a recession lasting a few years both volume and profitability would go down. They did.

During the war the heavy traffic of trooping and supply ships put the railway more or less back on its feet. In fact the war did better than that for it, for when peace came the railway ended up with a nice little nest-egg from the war compensation fund. As in so many undertakings, peace brought a considerable boom which enabled a dividend of 3% in 1919, based on a record 22,000,000 passengers. The speed of the subsequent collapse was remarkable: within two years the number of passengers was halved, and between 1920 and 1946 the ordinary shareholders received no dividends at all. The compensation money leaked quietly away in meeting the payments to the holders of preference shares, and in some years even those were delayed.

The ordinary shareholders were not best pleased about this state of affairs. They complained that there were too many directors drawing fees, and one humorist pointed out that they had slightly more than one director per route mile, which prompted another correspondent to the local press to suggest that if they had one per furlong things would be much better. Repeated attacks were launched on the salary of the General Manager. It has to be said that there was some justification: Cottrell was paid £2,200, which was indeed a large amount when compared with the salaries of senior officials of the Dock Board or the Corporation, whose responsibilities were far larger. Cottrell was at times allowed to take on paid outside work as well, and Neachell, his successor, was in poor health for several years before he retired. No slur is intended on either man, but each was paid a full-time salary when they were not in fact doing a full-time job. Not only did the company not pension Neachell off sick when they might have done, but they retained his services as a consultant at £500 pa when he finally did retire. This arrangement resulted in prolonged acrimony in successive AGMs, despite the fact that his successor,

who received only £1,600, was the one who was really paying Neachell's quasi-pension.

This was all great fun at AGMs and allowed lots of people to shout 'shame' at each other. A. T. Harding, perhaps the most persistent vilifier of the board (and of Neachell), was elected a director in 1929, by fellow dissenters who thought he could do them some good. Despite eventually becoming Chairman, his efforts, doubtless well-intended, made no difference whatever. Experiments like closing selected stations at 6.30pm were tried, which did make minor reductions in expenditure. The fact was that a few hundred pounds saved here or there was never going to make the railway profitable: the problems were much deeper-rooted than that. As it stood, the railway was only minimally viable, and to that stipulation must be added a second: while it stood.

It was the Accelerated Service which first drew attention to the potential problems of the structure. Its phenomenal acceleration, more than double that of the original trains, imposed strains which neither track nor structure would readily bear. The track life was reduced, and soon after the Accelerated Service began it was necessary to re-lay the track throughout.

The wear rate of the track on curves was particularly bad: while the straight bits in the protection of the tunnel lasted a dozen years or more, there were places on the curves where a rail lasted only a couple of years — and that figure was given by Rostron, long after the application of Neachell's flange-greasing machine had diminished wear on the curves. This indicates that the structure was probably suffering centrifugal overload as well. During the currency of the Accelerated Service, passengers complained of being thrown around on the curves at Alexandra. What this meant was that the ability of the high-powered units to accelerate to a higher speed from a standstill and their power to overcome the friction on curves allowed the imposition of much higher centrifugal loadings on those curves. The reaction to those G-forces which threw the passengers about went straight into the structure.

The Hobson decking contained the seeds of its own destruction. The original accounts of the design of the structure are at times ambiguous about which parts were iron and which steel. H. M. Rostron, the last General Manager, in his paper to the Liverpool Engineering Society in 1952, mentioned repairing damage to the decking by arc-welding steel patches onto it. It is true that it was possible in 1952 to weld steel to wrought iron by the use of the recently developed nickel alloy electrodes intended for repairing iron castings. They were not recommended for the purpose, nor recommended for use other than in the downhand position, and they were also phenomenally expensive. In general, wrought iron was not considered arc-weldable, and many welding engineers today would still prefer oxy-acetylene. We may therefore take it that the Hobson decking plates were of mild steel, which is more susceptible to producing large volumes of flaky scale than is wrought iron.

The location of the longitudinal sleepers on the decking was found wanting, with the result that they worked to and fro on the crowns of the Hobson decking. The wood being relatively soft, abrasive materials like wind-borne grit or particles of scale from the decking became embedded in it, with the result that the sleepers slowly but effectively sawed their way through the plating.

The sections of the structure were not, of course, fastened immovably to each other and to the columns, or strange and unpleasant things would have happened with changes in temperature. One end of each span rested 'free', secured by loose bolts in slots, on a sliding bearer, and we find that the bearers were wearing. This statement, made in a throw away manner, needs a little more consideration. If excessive acceleration and deceleration were wearing the bearer blocks, then the other end of the span must have been moving as well. How was it doing so? By flexing the columns? It is extremely unlikely that this motion could have arisen without working either rivets or bolts in their holes. In short, the faster and heavier trains overloaded the structure in terms of its longitudinal stiffness, and this damage was in effect permanent as Rostron's later description of arc-welded repairs to the bearer blocks shows.

From the top side, the decking presented a narrowing V-shaped crevice for harbouring moisture above the riveted joints. Only a diligently enforced regime of scraping out and re-coating with bitumen would prevent the occurrence of the inevitable. Once water got into those joints, of which there were thousands, corrosion between the vertical faces of

the Hobson plates would begin. When mild steel rusts, the rust it produces has a volume roughly 32 times that of the metal from which it came, and the expansion will produce pressures sufficient to buckle better plates than theirs. The corrosion was not only gradually removing metal, but also changing the profile of the Hobson plates, upon which the strength of the structure depended.

Meanwhile, underneath, the MD&HB's robust little tank locomotives were cheerfully anointing the structure with a high-pressure mix of hot water, assorted acids and abrasive particles. Oral information from an old Dock Board man tells of a good 'chuff' bringing down chunks of bituminous paint with the scale underneath still adhering to it.

It seems unlikely that the Company and its engineers could fail to realise that these were significant maintenance problems peculiar to a railway built almost entirely on a composite iron and steel viaduct. The Mersey Railway Company never tired of telling its shareholders how unlucky they were that their railway was down a deep hole and therefore had special problems of pumping, ventilation and lift provision. The LOR Chairman's Reports for the 1920s contain, as an article as unchangeable as the apologies for the poor financial results, the statement that the structure had been most carefully maintained with the very best paint (or was it the best butter?) and was in every respect as good as the day it was built. This last expression is a conventional form widely used in reports. Perhaps some of the shareholders believed it.

This line was purveyed until 1931. So late as 1927, a consulting engineer, namely Sir Gilbert Fox, had subscribed to the formula that the structure was effectively as good as new, but in 1931 a detailed report from Sir Douglas Fox & Partners modified this by the statement that considering the structure was 40 years old it was in very good condition. The scaling and painting regime was said to have

Right: This view has never been positively identified, but appears to show repairs after war damage, nearing completion. *IAL*

preserved about 90% of the structure very well, but the remaining 10%, being the awkward bits down cracks, under the track etc, were suffering exactly the problems suggested above. Words were not minced as the report spoke of the destruction of material in load-bearing members. Shareholders were told that those works described as requiring immediate attention were already in hand and the rest of the recommendations would be carried into effect over the next few years. We know what some of these works were: curved patches were being riveted onto the crowns of the Hobson plates where the sleepers had been wearing through them.

This raises interesting questions about the inspection regime of the railway. If the structure was, as the shareholders were assured, regularly scraped and painted with great care to maintain it in excellent condition, who made the decision to paint this or that part of it at any particular time, and on what basis? Box tells us that his father, when assistant to Neachell, used to travel the length of the track regularly, and inspect the generating station and the permanent way. Because these visits tended to be at the weekend, young Charles Box was able to accompany his father — and it seems to have been one of the highlights of his schooldays — so we have an eyewitness account. Box senior was, of course, a qualified engineer, albeit a mechanical rather than a civil. He had his own small permanent maintenance staff, so it seems extremely unlikely that he could be unaware of the deterioration which was going on. As anyone involved in the practical side of the railway preservation movement knows, one soon gets an eye for the presence of rust under paint, working rivets and wasted plates. The LOR men were doing this job full-time rather than just at weekends, and the suggestion that the Fox report came out of the blue strains the credulity of the reader. As a sidelight, we may recall that one of the defences offered against the attacks on Neachell's consultancy was the need to take advantage of his intimate knowledge of the structure. If it was all that intimate, he seems to have shared the fruits of his intimacy with very few people.

If the LOR did realise that there were real problems with the structure, then Rostron followed his predecessors in concealing the realisation, for in 1952 he explained to the Engineering Society that the company had recently carried out deflection tests which had revealed nothing amiss, and had had a small piece of one of the main girders analysed with eminently satisfactory results. The fact is that at least from Neachell's time, minor repairs had been going on to a structure which suffered from just about every possible problem except deterioration of the main girders of the spans.

This really was not good enough, for when the future of the railway was being considered by the Ministry for War Transport, and later by the Port Access Committee, it was common knowledge among insiders that the railway would need major structural attention soon after the end of the war. The Port Emergency Committee received plenty of paperwork between 1941 and 1945 to establish this, much of which survives. All the bodies involved considered it desirable that the LOR should continue in traffic, but they certainly did not imagine that it could run much longer on the basis of routine maintenance only. Not to put too fine a point on it, when Rostron gave his paper he was telling a load of porkies.

According to Box, the final chapter in the railway's history begins with the realisation in 1954 that the maintenance costs of the structure were becoming unacceptably high, which prompted the commissioning of a full investigation of its condition. It does not appear to have struck Box as odd that the report, which stated that enormous reconstruction was necessary, should come as a second bolt from the blue. Why should it, when just two years previously the General Manager had given a fairly upbeat account of the prospects of the railway? In the first place, Box is slightly misleading on the question of maintenance. In the early 1950s the sum spent annually on the structure varied in the region of £7,000–£8,000, which, allowing for inflation, was about the same as had been spent in the impoverished days of the mid-1930s, when the structure was some 50% younger. In the 1950s, larger sums were more readily affordable in that receipts were reasonably stable and the receipts to overall expenditure ratio was falling. Expenditure on maintenance of the structure was usually less than on that of the track and consistently much less than on 'repairs/partial renewals' of the stock. Further-more, annual expenditure on the structure actually fell by roughly a quarter after the end of the war.

The crisis which arose in 1954 was a fairly close re-enactment of the events of 1927–31. The same questions turn up again. How had the Company continued to operate a railway on a viaduct without knowing that much of its structure had seriously deteriorated? What inspection regime was in force? Clearly the structure was inspected fairly carefully, in order to programme the running repairs to the Hobson plates and the span bearers which Rostron described, and even if the objective was only to discover which bits were the worst it would be impossible not to discover accidentally which bits

94

Left: Now let's be honest, if someone proposed building a thing like that between three listed buildings nowadays we would all be up in arms. *IAL*

Below left: Southbound train leaving Pier Head in 1950. The building behind is the Mersey Tunnel ventilator and offices, still being repaired after war damage. This was the second building the LOR was bombed out of. *H. C. Casserley*

Right: This very similar view shows a different train but was taken by the same person, probably on the same day. Just legible on the further bus is a Government advert bearing the stern injunction 'Don't Waste Bread'. *H. C. Casserley*

Below: A cure for nostalgia: much of the time the LOR was cold, wet, dreary and uncomfortable for those who had to use it. And this was taken in August. *H. V. Booth*

were only very bad. The men whose job it was to carry out the repairs almost certainly knew this anyway, but the knowledge went astray somewhere between them and the shareholders. A new question also arises, which is why, even after the report had been received, the Company continued to spend roughly three times as much per year on face-lifting its antique rolling stock as it did on maintenance of the structure.

Was there, then, a hidden agenda intended to extract some money from the remains of the railway for its longsuffering shareholders, who were still only receiving a maximum of 3% in a good year? Profits began declining again and costs were said to be rising. In fact, rising costs were more a problem anticipated than encountered: the company paid pretty poor wages compared with British Railways and it was clear that sooner or later some measure of comparability would have to be conceded. The Company did not own land of any consequence, most of its premises being leasehold. Its material assets consisted of some workshop machinery, some rolling stock which we may safely assume that nobody (except possibly the City of Liverpool Museums) would want and a typewriter which, from surviving documents, appears to have been past the first flush of youth. It had no holdings in other companies apart from a few debentures which seem to have been notionally attached to the Renewal Fund (though this is not specifically stated in the accounts). The structure represented a large tonnage of scrap, but much of it was wrought iron, which nobody really wanted, and the difficulties of dismantling were such that it was doubtful whether there would be any net gain at the end. Had this not been the case, it might well have been cut up during the war.

We must remember that this was by no means the first time closure of the railway had been suggested or threatened. During the lean years of the early 1900s and again in the 1920s and 1930s there were those both inside and outside the company who believed the railway to be non-viable. Had it owned any really saleable assets it might well have been wound up as ordinary shareholders sought to cut their losses. As Maund has shown, there was a concerted campaign during World War 2, possibly orchestrated by the LMS, to have the LOR removed in order to provide better access for main-line trains to the docks. In particular, it was argued that the removal of the LOR would allow the addition of an extra line to the main line of the Dock Railway, substantially reducing the undoubted and acute congestion there. The campaign failed, partly because the LOR was desperately needed to sustain the frenzied workrate required throughout the dock system to sustain the war effort. This applied particularly at the graving docks, for the patching up of vessels which had limped in damaged after

surviving attacks on convoys. At least until late 1943 there were few higher strategic priorities than keeping the convoys moving.

Happily for the LOR and its supporters, the reconstruction of the dock railway with three lines would have caused protracted chaos, resulting in reduced rather than increased freight capacity for a considerable time. Nor were the men, the plant or the materials readily available. Nevertheless, one suspects that if sufficient buses and the fuel to run them could have been easily obtained, the LOR might have gone then. When all these difficulties were taken together with the small benefit to be gained from the scrap metal, neither the Port Emergency Committee in the first instance nor the Ministry for War Transport saw demolition of the Overhead as a risk worth taking.

The question of closure during the war would probably never have arisen had the railway been able to prove its indispensability by keeping running, but unfortunately it suffered heavy and repeated damage in the Blitz. For most of the duration of the war, attacks on Liverpool were infrequent and caused relatively little damage. Serious attacks began late in 1940 and the six days beginning 2 May 1941 saw an attack so sustained and intense in relation to the size and population of the city that Hughes has argued that Liverpool suffered greater proportionate losses than London or Coventry. This was a reflection of the Nazi realisation that the easiest way to sink a ship or destroy its cargo was not by going looking for it in the mostly deserted vastness of the North Atlantic and then fighting a convoy escort, but by bombing it in port.

Detailed accounts on an almost bomb-by-bomb basis have been published by Box and by Hughes, so for present purposes a summary of the worst incidents will suffice. On 31 August 1940, a bomb caused serious damage to one of the main girders south of James Street station while another caused lesser damage to the James Street bridge. On 26 September, part of the Wapping Warehouse collapsed onto the structure and buckled a span, and at Brunswick six spans were buckled by the heat from burning railway wagons and their loads on the rails below. It took until November to effect repairs. There followed a number of relatively trifling incidents which closed the railway or parts of it for short times, such as a further attack of rubble on the track at Wapping and another at Pier Head.

Just before Christmas, two spans were destroyed at Canada Dock, but by March it was once again possible to ride the whole length of the line — for about three days — before both tracks were cut near the bottom of 'The Switchback', but since none of the structure was involved, repairs were completed by 27 March and the line was again open right through — in good time for the Blitz proper, when three spans at James Street and three at Wapping were destroyed, James Street station was wrecked and so were the Company offices in James Street. Four spans at Canada were destroyed in two separate raids, and several more were badly shaken about by the explosion of the Malakand in Huskisson, with about 1,000 tons of high explosive aboard. The Company's temporary office in Tower Building was destroyed, forcing the unfortunate Box (Senior) to work once again from a train.

Every time a span came down, it blocked the main line of the dock railway, causing acute difficulty in moving cargoes along the dock estate. The repair work required quite large amounts of scarce steel and, being far beyond the capacity of the railway's tiny workshop staff, the employment of large numbers of skilled men provided by contractors. There were obviously going to be those who thought this a waste of resources, and the fact that parts of the route had been covered by buses for months at a time — it was not until November 1941 that the Overhead was fully back in action — proved that buses could do the job. Fortunately for the Overhead, it took about seven buses to carry a trainload of people and it also took them longer to make the journey, which meant that at peak times something like 60 buses would be needed and there were not 60 buses to be had. But as with the clandestine attacks by the railway's domestic enemies, it had been a close-run thing. Ironically, the war actually benefited the railway in revenue terms, for even in the 'darkest hour' of 1941 the railway took slightly over £80,000. While this was a significant fall from the £102,000 of 1940, it was more than the undamaged railway had earned in 1939, and in 1943 it rose to a very respectable £134,000.

Quite early on in the war, the Mayor of Bootle had suggested that the Overhead was an obstruction, and when it became clear that victory was only a matter of time, people's thoughts naturally turned to the brave new world which would be constructed as the Blitz damage was repaired. Among those were many who viewed the Overhead as a survival of a bygone world, half forgotten and half reviled. 'Victorian' was a term of abuse applicable in almost any context. In the understandable passion to look forward rather than back, people often failed to foresee the problems which excessive use of motor vehicles would bring. The bus, the lorry and the motor car appeared to be the obvious way forward, and it seems to have come as a genuine surprise that within five years of the closure of the Overhead the city's streets were hideously congested. Plans were produced involving the demolition of hundreds of acres of property to provide new roads. In particular, the City Council had a plan from as early as 1943 for

widening the Dock Road to 150ft, and kept a watching brief on any reconstruction work which might prejudice this. Had the LOR suffered any further damage late on in the war, it would have faced serious Corporation opposition to its repair.

It is only fair to add that even the Overhead's best friends could not deny that it was extremely ugly: old views of distinguished buildings like the Custom House seen from the Dock Estate make it clear that in one sense the eventual demolition of the railway was a blessing. It was to counter this 'old-fashioned and ugly' image that the directors took their apparently stupid decision to give the trains a facelift. While it may not have been the optimum course, it seems much less stupid when seen in its context.

There had been long-standing and reasonably successful attempts to market the railway as a tourist/educational trip to see the docks and the ships therein. These occasionally received a considerable boost from 'one-off' events such as the arrival of a major liner or warship in Gladstone Graving Dock or the capsizing in dock of the Empress of Canada. Reputedly the railway's busiest day ever was 19 July 1927, the Royal opening of Gladstone Dock. The fact remained that the railway served mainly as a way for dock workers to get to and from work and to move from one job on the Dock Estate to another. This was not high-value traffic.

But the Company did have something to sell. Its goodwill in the hard-nosed technical sense of the term was worth little, for its passenger revenue was low, although there was a slight recovery in both numbers and revenue towards the end. But there is another kind of goodwill, a non-technical and non-financial goodwill. This the LOR had not merely in abundance but to excess. It had become part of the fabric of life in a city which was always intensely proud and possessive of its own achievements. It was not until the 1970s that ferry commuters began to desert in critical numbers: in the late 1960s the boat deck was still occupied by a circular procession of businessmen taking the air. Throughout the journey, they walked round the deck, always clockwise, because it was part of the distinctive Merseyside way of life and travel. Any ordinary city like Manchester could have trams or buses. In the same way that the Mersey ferries were distinctive, so was the Overhead.

When once the possibility of the Overhead closing became public knowledge, this non-technical goodwill broke over it like a tidal wave. The image is deliberate: a tidal wave may cause damage, but it also represents a vast source of energy. That energy was soon applied to the question of saving the Overhead. Scouse loyalty surged onwards and upwards in torrents of nostalgia and invective.

The campaign to save a fictionalised Canterbury & Whitstable Railway in *The Titfield Thunderbolt* had nothing on this, apart from the fact that in films the goodies usually win, whereas in real-life railway history they hardly ever do.

This writer admits to being a jaded old cynic where railway finances are concerned. The Overhead had the skids under it almost from the start through being undercapitalised and built on the cheap. As time went by, trading conditions turned increasingly against it and essential maintenance was skimped. Even considerations of safety were if not positively neglected, at least given a priority, lower than many people would have thought wise or proper. This was not done for profit; nobody made any to speak of. It was done to minimise loss.

Despite the official story, it is highly improbable that those in the know did not realise by, at the absolute latest, 1950 that the railway was doomed. The actual figure needed for proper reinstatement of the structure may not have been known, but its rough order of magnitude must have been. That was all it was necessary to know, for the 1954 report spoke in terms of £2 million, of which about £1.6 million was for decking renewal. The MD&HB privately estimated it at £3 million. The Company had, of course, a renewal fund to handle just such an eventuality: it amounted to £176,165. £2 million was a laughable figure: about 2.25 times the existing share capital of the Company, 13 times the gross receipts and 80 times the net receipts. The dividend on ordinary shares was bumping along the bottom at around 0.5%, though in the last year of operation the Board asset-stripped the company to the tune of a 1.5% dividend. The raising of large sums of new capital was completely out of the question, and the only way the shareholders would see any money at all (and then not much) would be if the railway was taken over. That was where the wave of nostalgia and local pride came in.

Above: A few days before closure one of the modernised trains leaves Custom House station. *IAL*

Left: Rolling stock temporarily left in Herculaneum carriage shed. *C. E. Box*

Chapter 8
Closure

Virtually none of the information in the previous chapter was available to ordinary people at the time. Some of it, like the proceedings of the Port Emergency Committee was stamped 'secret', but even the company's shareholders were kept in the dark to what we would now think a surprising extent by the 'insiders'. The Shareholders' Minute Book is one of the comparatively small number of Company documents which survive, and merely to describe it as brief or perfunctory fails to convey an adequate impression of how little useful information it contains. From the extracts from discussions at AGMs published in the local press, it is clear that, although the shareholders could and did get quite stroppy at times, they really knew very little about the inner workings of their company — or about the state of the structure.

In that sense the impression Box gives of the threat of imminent closure coming as a surprise is not unreasonable. To those with no connection at all with the Company there had been no grounds for concern. Liverpool was a proud city: it had survived the war, it was rebuilding, business in the port was booming. The ferry boats had been old and rusting, and new ones were being built. Sentiments like these sell newspapers, and the local press was full of enthusiasm for the reinstatement of the railway. A good issue like that not only sells papers, but makes lots of people write to the editor to give the world the benefit of their opinions: it's free copy.

Behind the froth in the press, there were five basic ways in which the railway could imaginably have been saved. The first was so unlikely that we may discount it, as it was almost entirely discounted at the time, which was to restructure the Company, or form a new one, and carry on more or less as before. The Company had been a proven long-term loser for investors and the idea of finding £2 million was strictly for the fairies. Not a great deal more likely was the nationalisation of the railway. While the Conservative Government in power at the time was not making active moves to privatise the things the Attlee Government had nationalised, their desire to extend nationalisation was obviously limited. Their advisors would scarcely be enthusiastic about a small line which functionally if not operationally more resembled a tramway than a proper railway, which still ran from nowhere in particular to nowhere else and needed £2 million for starters.

Much hope was pinned upon the Dock Board. Their trade was doing very well and the dues were rolling in. The LOR was a considerable assistance to the work of the docks, so why should they not take it over? The Board had difficulty in winning hearts and minds on this one; indeed they attracted considerable local odium for a short while, because they could not tell the truth. The truth was that despite its apparent opulence, the Board had never had enough funds available for investment in what we now call 'core activities' since about 1900. Boast how they might about the extent of their estate, considerable areas of it were in dire need of modernisation and there were parts where war damage had not yet been reinstated.

Now the members of the Board had occasionally made stupid decisions and some of their management and working methods were archaic and wasteful, but they had known for many decades that whatever else went wrong the one thing they could never, ever, risk was their reputation for financial reliability and probity. Major engineering works were running (as usual) behind schedule and over budget and larger and costlier new works were known to be needed. The takeover of the LOR would have been of dubious legality (for the Board was still governed by the 1857 Act mentioned in Chapter 1) and it would be a certain loser. If they took it on it would be an ongoing revenue loss, but far more to the point, it would have been seriously damaging to their financial credibility when next they needed to borrow megabucks, which there was no doubt they would within a few years.

Unable to level with the press or the public, they repeatedly issued dead-bat statements in 1950s management-speak about how they were not a railway company and could not become one. Joe Public saw the little green locos with 'MD&HB' painted on the side and thought them liars. The benefit the Board derived from the availability of the LOR for moving port workers about was dismissed on the grounds that no other port authority spent money on facilities for its men to get to and from work, so there was no reason why they should. This appeared as mean-minded, and there were even those who pointed out that some Welsh slate quarries (organisations not generally distinguished by their coddling of their workers) ran passenger vehicles on their mineral lines to take their men to

work. The unspoken truth of the matter was that the Board knew the LOR was a financial plug-hole and it simply did not have the money to pour down it.

Liverpool Corporation in the 1950s was a very large and powerful body. Its annual budget was around £60 million per year, a sum we could multiply by about 20 or so to translate into modern prices for the things on which it spent most of its money. Obviously it could afford to take over the Overhead — or so it seemed to outsiders. In fact matters were very different.

Ever since Liverpool appointed the country's first Medical Officer of Health and first Borough Engineer (in 1846 and 1847 respectively) the city had struggled with a backlog of housing improvement. The war had made this task incomparably more difficult through diverting revenue to other works and rendering large numbers of comparatively poor people homeless. As a result, the City had been spending huge amounts on municipal housing at the expense even of rebuilding its own damaged properties. In 1955 the City Libraries and Museums were still heavily war-damaged, with large areas closed, and a considerable part of the roof of St George's Hall was of corrugated iron. A substantial area of Corporation-owned land in the office and commercial quarter was in use for car parking because there was no money for reconstruction.

As the new housing was built, naturally it spread outwards, because the substandard housing it replaced was of unacceptably high density. This created public transport problems, to which the Corporation had to find an answer. There are many who think it chose wrongly, but the fact is that the choice it made was to do away with trams and pin its faith on large-scale road improvements and lots of buses.

Local councillors needed people's votes, so when it seemed that there was a huge groundswell of popular support for the Overhead there were obviously going to be some who would espouse the cause. The Corporation was the principal objector to the Bill for closure, but since there was no serious money on offer, its objections were just so much wasted legal expense. These centred on the suggestion in an engineer's report that it would be possible to patch up the structure sufficient to last

another 10 years for the sum of about £250,000. That too was far beyond what they were willing to put in, although the road improvements and bus purchases to replace the Overhead would cost over £400,000 in capital, with an ongoing annual revenue loss of over £40,000. That £40,000 alone was, of course, more than the interest cost of bailing out the Overhead according to the figures they had paid their consultant to produce.

The reality of the matter is that it was largely the intervention of Corporation tramways which made the Overhead non-viable to begin with and the Corporation's current vision of the future of passenger transport centred on roads and buses. Whatever soft words it might utter, and however much money it might waste in empty pretence of 'saving the railway', the likelihood of it putting any money into the LOR was, in the words of George Bush 'Zilch, zero, zed'. It wanted it shut. Bootle Borough Council, which was not rich enough for decisive intervention anyway, followed a similar policy.

The final possibility which was mooted is laughable. A handful of people came up with the idea that there ought to be a new public body, to be called something like the Merseyside Transport Authority, which would mould all existing passenger services, with perhaps some new ones added, into a coherent metropolitan system. In such a system, the LOR would be a valuable link (shades of the 'Belt Route' again) and the costs of its repair could be spread around the network in exactly the way that large railway companies used to spread major repair costs. As any transport historian knows, this is simply not the way things are meant to work. New 'services' are only provided in desperation, in the unfortunate circumstance of there being no existing service from which to try to gain traffic. Competitive, not complementary, services were the historical norm, and any idea that services should co-operate to form a coherent system was the sort of utopian rubbish that Mussolini had tried to force on people. He is even said to have made the trains run to time, and look where it got him.

Ultimately, the Merseyside Passenger Transport Executive was established with a brief to establish just such a co-ordinated system, and it burrowed under central Liverpool to unite the tracks of the former L&YR and CLC. That link fulfils the function in the Merseyrail system which a restored LOR would have done. The problem with the MPTE was that after a certain gestation period it was beginning to show signs of achieving its objective of an integrated system, which is why it was abolished. It could no more buck the underlying assumptions of British transport policy over the last 150 years than could the Overhead.

Above left: Demolition began at the southern end. This view is just north of Herculaneum (new) station, looking north. *IAL*

Left: The first section of the overhead structure being demolished just north of Herculaneum, September 1957. *Liverpool Daily Post*

Above: Loading sections of Hobson decking for scrap, at the bottom of James Street. *IAL*

Above right: A similar view about 100yd further on. *IAL*

Charles Box, I have recently realised, was guilty of misleading his readers over the chances of the LOR surviving. He was an engineer and a gentleman, so he lacked the insight of the embittered historian who can identify the apparent fairy godmother as being Rosa Klebb in disguise. He trusted journalists and politicians. He gave the impression, for example, that the failure of the Corporation to do anything to save the railway was down to party divisions. It was not: the objections to the closure had cross-party support, as did the refusal to put any money where the municipal mouth was. Rostron was less naïve, and tried to con public bodies — any public body — into buying a rusting liability. He even offered to give it away, and anyone who has seen the strictures on wilful neglect of maintenance contained in Brigadier Parkman's report will know why. While Rostron may have avoided overrating their integrity, he underrated their intelligence. Once the state of the structure became public knowledge, the railway was dead.

The obsequies were long and fairly painful. The seemingly mandatory public meetings were held and worthless pledges of support given and received. The intensity of press coverage attracted by the proposed closure of the railway ensured that every Council or Parliamentary starlet had to have their say. The Act

for the closure of the line eventually received the Royal Assent on 2 August 1956. An amendment to the original Bill had been incorporated to the effect that while the line could close on 30 December that year, another nine months must elapse before demolition began, to provide time for possible further rescue bids. More meetings were held and sundry other bodies tut-tutted about closure. Talk was cheap and the repair of the structure was not.

Statutory notices of closure were posted in late November. It is interesting to note that the urge to take a last ride on railways which are about to be closed was presumably already in existence then, as the Company prudently increased its fares in October. The last day was a dismal and occasionally wet Sunday, but all the trains were heavily loaded with people bidding farewell: the locals to an old friend and railway enthusiasts from further afield to the pioneer of the electric multiple unit.

The closure time stipulated in the Act was midnight, and trains ran right through the evening,

the ceremonial last trains departing simultaneously from Dingle and Seaforth, one of original 1893 stock and the other of modernised stock. The LOR would have no further need of its stock of fog detonators, so they were laid in lines on the track for these last trains to set off like so many graveside salutes. At least two of the men on duty that night had worked on the Overhead since before World War 1. There were photographs, there were even a couple of people with newfangled devices like cine cameras and tape recorders. There were flowers, and Box touchingly records that Driver Fawcett (of the last northbound train) was presented with a bouquet of chrysanthemums from 'The Murphys, of Bevington Bush'. Bevington Bush is a street just off Scotland Road then inhabited (for in those days sectarian and occupational divisions still lingered on) mostly by Roman Catholics who worked on the docks. What made people who lived in pretty severe poverty send flowers they almost certainly could not afford for a dead railway? We are in the heartland of Scouse legend.

The reality is that long before the Murphys' chrysanthemums had wilted, the power was turned off and so was most of the ageing workforce. For over half a century the Corporation had wanted control of passenger transport on the Dock Road:

now it had it. As one might expect, the new bus routes were slower, less convenient and more expensive. It was a bit embarrassing that within a few months the Suez crisis left the buses short of diesel fuel, but embarrassment containment is the stuff of politics. The main objective — control — was won.

But we have forgotten, have we not, that the railway was to be left standing to allow further rescue bids. It is not recorded whether the author of that provision was injured by a flying pig, but anyone who believed that the railway could be revived once the buses had started was certainly running that risk. In whose interest would such a thing be? Only of the likes of the Murphys of Bevington Bush who, in the dark days before the National Lottery, did not have £2 million to spare. Whether anyone believed this outrageous sham is unclear, but the delay in demolition did not modify in the slightest the statement made above that once the state of the LOR structure become public knowledge, the railway was dead.

Box also tells us that by the time further meetings were held on the possibility of rescuing the Overhead, the feasibility of this happening had been reduced by what he termed 'theft and vandalism'. However, the Company had been accused of

Above: A bit further north again, on the right is a main girder awaiting cutting down to truckable length. *IAL*

Below: Demolishing Pier Head station in November 1957. *Liverpool Daily Post*

removing equipment shortly after the line closed. Their response was that they were removing various items, including clocks, to places of safety to prevent theft and vandalism. Among the things allegedly destroyed by the (unofficial) vandals were the clocks which were not there. Whether in good faith or bad, the Company had given a moral *carte blanche* for looters, and when people who worked on the docks saw something they used and valued left abandoned, they did not retain a very strong idea of the sanctity of property. They probably considered themselves quite justified in liberating quantities of copper and other desirable substances. Considerable damage was said to have occurred in the process, and the directors were quite understandably concerned that they might be held liable for any resultant accidents to innocent members of the public. The simple fact was that they wanted out as soon as possible. There was no prospect of a last-minute rescue, so they applied for authority to demolish the structure immediately. Although this was obtained, there was some delay in signing the contract, and work did not actually begin until September.

Nearly all the stock had been stored in the Dingle Tunnel and shortly after closure it was moved under its own power to Seaforth Sands. The crews which moved the trains were shuttled back in another train. There were 54 units left, of which a rebuilt motor and trailer (Nos 14 and 7) were sold and No 3, which was almost completely original, was acquired for the Liverpool City Museums (now National Museums & Galleries on Merseyside). The remaining 51 units found no buyers and from July onwards were gradually broken up in the carriage shed at Seaforth. At the instigation of Charles Box, the body of No 7 was eventually rescued from its role as a temporary building, and taken to Steamport, at Southport, for preservation.

At this time the company was still in business, but on 30 September 1957 liquidators were appointed to begin the complicated task of winding up. They must have generated a huge amount of fascinating paperwork, most of which was destroyed shortly afterwards, just a few items like the Shareholders' Minute Book and a volume of published annual accounts being presented to the Liverpool Record Office. The final distribution to shareholders, of 9s 1d, was not announced until 26 September 1960.

The replacement bus service was not immediately popular. The Dock Road was just as congested in 1956 as it had been when people first decided that it was necessary to build the Overhead. In two respects it was worse, in that it was a reasonably frequent occurrence to meet longish trains crossing the

105

Dock Road, travelling, as was required, at walking pace and accompanied by a flagman. There were times when there were simply too many lorries trying to get to a particular berth to be able to find space for them to wait inside the Dock Estate. This rarely happens nowadays because everyone has become better at logistics, but if it does, lorries can wait on the former line of the Dock Railway. When that was in use they could not, and the wartime practice of allowing them to wait in the middle of the road was continued. This prevented overtaking, and there was still some very slow traffic around, including a small number of horse-drawn vehicles.

Clearly the buses would be unbelievably slow if they used the Dock Road. Apart from the congestion, it was in dire need of resurfacing, so for nearly all the length of the route they used the next available parallel road inland, which in some cases was several hundred yards away. In this way they contrived to take only about 5min longer than the trains — if one neglected the walking time. Overall, the increases in fares were not outrageous, but every fare increased and in particularly unfavourable cases, such as Huskisson and Seaforth return, the fare doubled.

The demolition of the structure was not a particularly difficult task technically, for most of it could be cut up with oxy-acetylene into pieces which could be craned down onto lorries. Work began at Herculaneum, where there was plenty of working space at ground level. In those circumstances it was possible to cut up and carry away spans at the rate of more than one per day, but there were nearly 600 of them and it was not nearly so easy to remove them when obstruction of traffic below had to be minimised. The demolition gangs obviously improved with practice, for by the end of January 1959 the job was finished. There does not seem to be a definitive record of the weight of metal involved: the 'demolitionists' of 1941 had claimed there was 65,000 tons, while Greathead and Fox stated that the weight of the original length of structure was about 20,000. Perhaps Neachell and his successors had put on more patches than we realised.

People often enquire of anyone known to be interested in the history of the Overhead whether it should have been saved. It is not an easy one to answer, but on balance it seems that one must regretfully answer 'no'. In the short term the loss of the Overhead caused difficulty and expense to employers in and around the Dock Estate and to people travelling to work or calling on business there. When A. E. Smith Coggins, Master Stevedores, wound up, the loss of the Overhead as a quick cheap means of moving gangs of men from

Above left: The scene at Seaforth Sands where stock was broken up. There seems to be no attempt to recover materials — expensive aluminium panels are just strewn about — much less to maintain any pretence of workshop practice. *IAL*

Above: No, it's not a shiny new bus replacing the LOR, it's a rather tired one. It would be nice to know what the conductor is gesticulating about. *IAL*

one berth to another was mentioned as a factor in their failure. In the longer term, the entire structure of the port and its associated industries would change so much within 15 years of closure that the railway would have faced bankruptcy again. In the 1950s there were some 25,000 registered dock workers: today more tonnage is moved through the port with under 500. A high proportion of the business is done in just two docks, Royal Seaforth and Gladstone, and there are no operational docks south of Bramley-Moore. Most of the jobs on the docks are now specialised, so that the movement of gangs of men between widely separated berths is unusual. The scale of ship-repairing activities is, by the standards of former times, tiny.

Along the other side of the Dock Road, not one of the railway depots is still working. Such imports as leave by rail (mainly coal, bulk grain and containers) go direct from the quaysides of Royal Seaforth and Gladstone and exports arrive by the same route. Since Liverpool gained Freeport status the fast-dwindling amount of general warehousing outside the estate has virtually vanished: this all happens inside the fence now with, relatively speaking, only a handful of men, most of them fork-lift drivers. The number of clerks in small quayside offices is much reduced by simplified procedures, computerisation and the removal of the Dock Offices from Pier Head to Seaforth. The people are simply not there to use the Overhead.

Liverpool's population has also been significantly reduced, first by the madcap policies of the 1960s which encouraged people to move to outlying towns or to new towns. 'Overspill' they were called. Then, in the late 1970s and early 1980s, came a wave of closures of major factories costing tens of thousands of jobs. The situation is improving slowly, but Liverpool is still one of the easiest cities in which to commute, whether by car or by public transport, because there are fewer people travelling to work than the road and rail systems were designed to cope with. When we look to the Overhead's ride-to-work catchment areas, only Dingle, Herculaneum and Seaforth & Litherland stations would now attract much traffic.

It is true that, mainly under the aegis of the Merseyside Development Corporation, there is now a considerable amount of new business and tourist trade in the former south docks. But although millions of people visit the south docks for business or pleasure, it is unlikely that they would find the Overhead useful if it were still there: it was designed for moving along the waterfront, not getting to and from it. Not only does the same apply to the people who live in flats in converted warehouses, but it is open to question whether the Wapping and Waterloo warehouses would have made very desirable residences with trains rumbling by at first floor level. It is just conceivable that it might have been connected to BR at Edge Hill via the two closed tunnels to the docks, but finding the space for the approach viaducts would have been nearly as difficult as finding the money. And who would do that in the age of the motor car?

The time may be coming when some form of public transport to do the job of the Overhead could be wanted again, and no doubt if that happens there will be a chorus of denunciation of its demolition. But who would have paid its losses, to which the interest on £2 million would have been only the overture, for the last 40 years? The sad fact is that at the crunch point in 1956, the Company, the Dock Board, the Corporation and the Ministry of Transport were unanimous in wanting rid of it. Ironically, the Dock Board was the only one of these bodies which followed a logical and honest policy, and collected the flak for it. Like I said, in railway history the goodies, be they the Dock Board or the Murphys of Bevington Bush, hardly ever win.

Left: A No 1 bus turning onto the Dock Road at the bottom of Canning Place. The empty site to the left is where the Custom House stood. *IAL*

Below: There is a vicious irony in this picture: in 1957 passenger travel along the docks was reduced almost to the condition which had first prompted John Grantham, more than a century before, to propose... an overhead railway. *IAL*

Appendices

Station and Distances

Station No.	Station	Station to Station in yds.	Total Miles	yds.
1	Seaforth and Litherland	0	-	-
2	Seaforth Sands	1,047	-	1,047
3	Gladstone Dock	708	-	1,755
4	Alexandra Dock	782	1	777
5	Langton Dock	300	1	1,077
6	Brockleband Dock	396	1	1,473
7	Canada Dock	1,068	2	781
8	Huskisson Dock	557	2	1,338
9	Sandon Dock	160	2	1,498
10	Nelson Dock	623	3	361
11	Clarence Dock	446	3	807
12	Princes Dock	1,026	4	73
13	Pier Head	792	4	865
14	James Street	330	4	1,195
15	Custom House (renamed Canning)	274	4	1,469
16	Wapping Dock	808	5	517
17	Brunswick Dock	742	5	1,259
18	Toxteth Dock	701	6	200
19	Herculaneum (new station)	633	6	833
20	Herculaneum (old station)	165		
21	Dingle	1,087	7	160

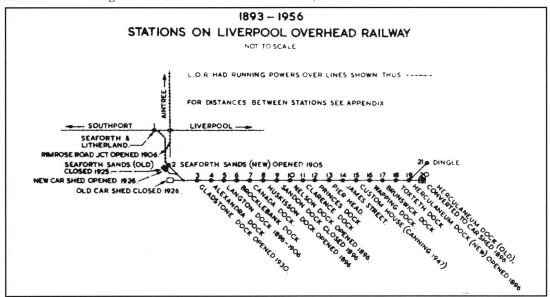

Make-up and seating capacity of LOR trains as at early 1956

Coach Nos	1st	3rd	Total
1-13-22	36	96	132
2-1-9	40	116	156
3-17-13	40	116	156
4-47-17w	38	204	242
5-15-11	36	96	132
6-48-10w	38	204	242
7-16-19w (exc 16)	40	158	198
8-14-24	36	96	132
10-4-12	36	96	132
14-7-30	36	84	120

Coach Nos	1st	3rd	Total
15-12-16	36	88	124
18-5-29	36	96	132
21-11-23w	40	154	194
25-10-27w	48	150	198
26-9-28	36	96	132
39-3-40	40	112	152
41-2-42	40	112	152
43-6-44	40	112	152
45-8-46	40	112	152

w = wide coach

Trailer coaches

	1-8
Builder	Brown Marshall in 1895
Length over body	32ft
Length over buffers	34ft 6in
Width over body	8ft 6in
Height — rail to roof top	11ft $^5/_8$in
Seating Second class	
First class	40
Centre buffers	large type
Westinghouse air brakes	8 blocks
Pressed steel bogie frames	Fox's patent
Bogie centres	20ft
Wheels dia	2ft 9in
Bogie wheelbase	7ft
Weight	13 ton 12cwt

Above: Lively Polly with a spare bogie frame coupled, delivering some rails. This shot also shows her ice-cutting shoe very clearly. *IAL*

Trailer No 5 lost in Dingle fire on 23-12-1901 .

From 1914 the LOR converted from two- to three-car trains and the following trailer coaches were added.

No 5	1914	1st class	Built by LOR as standard trailer	
9	1916	1st	MCC&W as standard trailer	
10	1917	1st	as wide trailer	
11	1917	1st	as wide trailer	
47	1918	3rd		45ft long 3ft wheels
48	1918	3rd	as wide trailer	45ft long 3ft wheels
12	1932	1st	LOR as standard trailer from motor coach	
13	1933	1st		
14	1933	1st		
15	1934	1st		
16	1935	1st		
17	1936	1st		

Specification of Locomotives

	Lively Polly	Ruston diesel
	0-4-0T	0-4-0
Built by	Kitson & Co Ltd, Leeds	Ruston & Hornsby Ltd
Date	1893	1947
Length over buffers	15ft 11in	17ft 8in
buffer beams	12ft	
Overall width	8ft 5in	7ft 5in
Height from rail to cab top	9ft 4in	10ft $^3/_8$in
Wheel dia	3ft	2ft 6in
Wheelbase	6ft	5ft 2$^3/_4$in
Cylinders	2 @ 12in by 8in	Four
Boiler dia	2ft 9in	
Heating surface	136.5sq ft	
Grate area	6.4sq ft	
Working pressure	150lbs per sq in	
Tank capacity	200 gall	
Tractive effort	2,720 1b	44bhp at 1,000rpm
Weight in working order	10ton 2cwt	7ton 10cwt

Motor Coaches

	1-30	31-38	39-46	L&YR Nos 1000-1011 (later LMSR 11700-11711) Dingle cars
Builder	*Brown Marshall*	*Brown Marshall*	*Brown Marshall*	*L&Y*
	in 1891	in 1893	in 1895	in 1905
Length over body	45ft	40ft	40ft	45ft
Length over buffers	47ft 2in	42ft 6in	42ft 6in	
Width over body	8ft 6in	8ft 6in	8ft 6in	9ft 6in
Height - rail to roof top	11ft $^5/_8$in	11ft $^5/_8$in	11ft $^5/_8$in	12ft 3$^3/_8$in
Seating Second class	41	41	57	50
First class	16	16		20
Drivers compt. small	5ft by 3ft	5ft by 8ft 6in	5ft by 8ft 6in	
Centre buffers	small type	large type	large type	
Westinghouse air brakes	6 blocks	6 blocks	6 blocks	
Gearless motor	60hp (front axle)	60hp (front axle)	70hp (front axle)	2@1 25hp
Pressed steel bogie frame	Fox's patent	Fox's patent	Fox's patent	
Bogie centres	32ft	27ft	27ft	32ft
Wheel dia	2ft 9in	2ft 9in	2ft 9in	3ft 6in
Bogie wheelbase	7ft	7ft	7ft	7ft
Weight of motor + axle - wheels	3 ton	3 ton	3 ton 17cwt	
motor bogie complete	5 ton 7cwt	5 ton 7cwt	6 ton 4cwt	
electrical equipt.	6 ton 7cwt	6 ton 7cwt	6 ton 17cwt	
of complete motor coach	20 ton	18½ ton	19 ton	22 ton

Nos 4, 6, 7, 17, 19, 20, 21, 23, 25, 27 rebuilt Brown
Marshall in 1902/3 to width of 9ft 4in with full width
drivers compartment and seating 60 second class and 19 first class.

Bibliography

This is not an academic publication, but the Overhead was an interesting and important little railway which a few readers might feel inspired to get to know more about, hence this outline of where the author found his information.

1. Original Material.
Because the LOR was twice bombed out of its offices, very little pre-war archive material survives. The most convenient source for Company meetings, accidents and major events on the railway is Newscuttings File No 99 in the MD&HB archive at Merseyside Maritime Museum. This collection also contains papers from the Port Emergency Committee and various other items relating to the LOR, including A. G. Lyster's report on American Overhead Railways and a small amount of Parliamentary material. For the truly diligent, more detailed accounts of the business side are to be found in Herapath's *Railway Journal* and on the technical side in *The Engineer* and *Engineering* for dates which are evident from the main text.

Some record material made its way into the Liverpool City Record Office (within the Central Library). There are two main deposits, one from Willans (principal contractor for the construction) and one from the liquidators. There is a relatively small amount of material in the Public Record Office, mainly about the wartime problems mentioned above, and the proceedings of the various Parliamentary Committees which deliberated on the Railway's different Bills, including the Closure Bill, are in the House of Lords Record Office. (You don't have to be a Lord: ordinary mortals are allowed in by appointment.)

2. Secondary works.
The standard reference work is C. E. Box, *The Liverpool Overhead Railway,* published by Ian Allan and their predecessors in various editions from 1957 to 1984. There is a huge amount of information, much of it based on personal experience, to the point where one unkind reviewer of the first edition considered that it contained unnecessary detail! There is also information about the LOR's tramway to Crosby, which has been omitted from this book.

Because of the shortage of original record material, Box relied heavily on the four professional engineering papers mentioned below, and they, to some extent, relied on each other. The time was ripe for some revisionist history, and a Research Dayschool at Merseyside Maritime Museum on 13 November 1993

provided this, with five papers, listed below. These give further and more detailed references. (Available as a Xerox-produced comb-bound booklet from the Museum, currently £2 + p&p.)

There are also two lighter-weight works on the railway, namely John Gahan's cheerfully anecdotal *Seventeen Stations to Dingle,* Birkenhead, 1982, and Paul Bolger's excellent picture-book *The Dockers' Umbrella,* Liverpool, 1993.

The definitive work on the Liverpool Blitz (including, obviously, its effects on the LOR) is J. C. Hughes, *Port in a Storm,* Liverpool, 1993.

3. Professional or academic papers.
J. H. Greathead & F. Fox, 'The Liverpool Overhead Railway', *Minutes of the proceedings of the Institution of Civil Engineers* Vol CXVII (1894), pp 51–70.

T. Parker, 'The Electrical Equipment of the Liverpool Overhead Railway' ibid, pp 71–83.

Discussion and correspondence on the above, ibid, pp 85–122.

E. J. Neachell, 'Notes on the Overhead Railway', *Transactions of the Liverpool Engineering Society,* Vol XXXVII (1915-16) pp 47–55. Discussion of the above together with a paper on the Mersey Railway, ibid pp 74–85.

H. M. Rostron, 'The Liverpool Overhead Railway — a Pioneer in Rapid Transit', *Transactions of the Liverpool Engineering Society* Vol LXXIII (1951–52) pp 89–121. (Including discussion)

P. Rees (ed), *Liverpool Overhead Railway,* 1893-1956, Liverpool, 1994, contains the following papers:

J. C. Hughes, 'The Pre-history of the Liverpool Overhead Railway.'
M. C. Duffy, 'Electric Rapid-transit Railways, 1890-1920.'
A. Jarvis, 'The Liverpool Overhead Railway and the Dock Board.'
G. Woodward, 'The Liverpool Overhead Railway: Innovations in Engineering.'
T. B. Maund, 'The Liverpool Overhead Railway's Secret War: the Battle With the Bureaucrats.'

112